W9-BNF-389

"Robby Dawkins has written a very interesting book on 'doing the stuff.' I loved the inspiring stories, as well as the practical insight into how to hear from God and relay what He is showing you to others. A very interesting, inspiring and encouraging book."

Randy Clark, founder and president,
The Apostolic Network of Global Awakening

"Robby is an example of a laid-down lover who understands that Kingdom power is rooted in God's love. *In Do What Jesus Did*, he imparts the nonnegotiable value of God's presence over everything else. The testimonies he releases are sure to stir up fearless love in each one of us."

Heidi Baker, Ph.D., founder, Iris Global

"The readers of this book are in for a ride. The pages are full of faith-building stories, and you the reader will find yourself asking, "Really? Did that really happen? Did he really do this or that?" I have known Robby for many years, and I have watched him actually live out what he is sharing in these pages. Allow your heart to be challenged and empowered so each can go and do likewise."

Phil Strout, national director, Vineyard USA

"As I read *Do What Jesus Did*, I felt a fresh call of the Spirit to grab hold of the Kingdom and to allow His life to flow through me. If you hunger for an awakening, open here and feast."

Steve Sjogren, author, *Conspiracy of Kindness*; Kindness.com

"Robby Dawkins reminds me in many ways of the apostle Peter. He is one of those rare individuals who is willing to step out from the safety of the boat and try to walk on water toward Jesus. Like Peter's story, Robby's contains times of near-drowning, but he also knows the thrill of doing what few Christians even attempt to do: not only proclaim the Kingdom of God but also demonstrate the Kingdom. *Do What Jesus Did* will encourage you to step out of your boat and take risks for the sake of Christ's Kingdom."

Rich Nathan, senior pastor, Vineyard Columbus

DO
WHAT
JESUS
DID

DO WHAT JESUS DID

a real-life field guide
to healing the sick,
routing demons and
changing lives forever

ROBBY DAWKINS

Chosen

a division of Baker Publishing Group
Minneapolis, Minnesota

© 2013 by Robert Dawkins

Published by Chosen Books
11400 Hampshire Avenue South
Bloomington, Minnesota 55438
www.chosenbooks.com

Chosen Books is a division of
Baker Publishing Group, Grand Rapids, Michigan

Printed in the United States of America

Library of Congress Cataloging-in-Publication Data

Dawkins, Robby.
    Do what Jesus did : a real-life field guide to healing the sick, routing demons, and changing lives forever / Robby Dawkins.
        pages cm.
    Includes bibliographical references.
    Summary: "A Chicago pastor offers a real-life field guide to healing the sick, routing demons, and making a dynamic impact for the Kingdom of God"—Provided by publisher.
    ISBN 978-0-8007-9557-3 (pbk. : alk. paper)
    1. Evangelistic work. 2. Missions. 3. Miracles. 4. Demonology. 5. Spiritual healing. I. Title.
BV3790.D4155 2013
269′.2—dc23   2013002788

Cover design by Gearbox

14 15 16 17 18 19   7 6 5 4 3 2

This book is dedicated to the memory of the loving life and ministry of my mother, Rose Marie Douglas Dawkins. Her love for Jesus and her selfless sacrifice for me and many others whom she pastored and led have shaped my life forever. Time and again, I saw her reach out and serve people, including the homeless and mentally ill in our home. In the early seventies, many runaways and homeless teens found a mother's loving arms in her embrace. We took so many people in whom she would love, cook for and share Jesus' life-changing message with. Her faith and relationship with Jesus were unshakable. Even in her final days of battling painful colon cancer, she turned to me one night and said, "Jesus' loving-kindness is better than life."

The story of my birth illustrates my mom's faithfulness to God. Satan appeared to her and told her that if she allowed my birth to take place, he would kill both of us when I was born. My mom's response was, "The Lord clearly has a plan for this child's life that you want to stop, and I will not put my hand against God's plan—even if it means the loss of my own life." From that day on, she battled regular visitations and torment from Satan as he tried to get her to terminate the pregnancy. Her answer was always firm; she would not do it. I was born on Easter Sunday morning. Though there had never been any complications during her pregnancy with me, as the doctor departed the delivery room he turned to my father and said,

"I just left a war zone. Both mother and child are fine, but it wasn't without a fight." I believe that occurred because of what is contained for you within the pages of this book.

Special Thanks

I also want to thank my wonderful wife, Angie, and six sons, Judah, Micah, Isaiah, Elijah, Canah and Caspian, for their undying support and patience in this process. You seven are all my inspiration.

I want to especially thank Nicole Voelkel, without whom this project would have never happened. Her research, writing and passion for the message in this book were so significant. I am forever appreciative of her faithful dedication.

Contents

Foreword

One of my favorite Bible stories is about the two disciples walking on the road to Emmaus. Jesus had just died, and to say they were disappointed would be the understatement of the century. Jesus had brought hope to every area of life, and now that hope was dead.

A stranger joined them as they walked along the road. He began to share his insights about the Messiah and His need to suffer on behalf of humanity. The disciples were so moved that they persuaded him to stay with them at their destination. When they sat down to eat, the man took bread and broke it. In that moment their eyes were opened. It had been Jesus the whole time. He was resurrected! And as quickly as He was revealed, He disappeared.

Their discussion following His departure is what moves me most. When referring to His conversation with them, they said, "Didn't our hearts burn within us?"

My heart began to burn while reading Robby Dawkins' *Do What Jesus Did*. I know of no other way to explain it. My heart burns with passion, hope and the wonder of what could become of my life with this book in hand. His miracle stories carry the

DNA of the resurrected Christ. What moves me most is Jesus performing supernatural works through very natural people.

I had an interesting experience while reading this book. On one page my heart would leap over the story of a miracle—because of both the redemptive work of Jesus and the courage of the author. On the next page my heart would leap over Robby's wisdom and insights as seen in his approach to a situation or to the Scriptures themselves. This book is filled with wisdom and testimonies—both of which are great treasures to believing believers.

While pondering this, I remembered Psalm 19:7: "The testimony of the LORD is sure, making wise the simple" (NASB). That powerful combination of testimonies and wisdom adds stability to every follower of Jesus. Many look at the pursuit of a life of miracles as random, careless and suspect. Biblically, however, the testimony of the miraculous is *sure*—meaning stable and supportive. Stories of miracles bring the stability of wisdom into the life of the believer. And this book presents this reality beautifully.

I have the feeling spiritual giants will emerge at the reading of *Do What Jesus Did*, because something gets awakened in the hearts of believers that has been either bruised by disappointments or buried by lies. Robby does a marvelous job of letting the reader know that if he can walk in a miracle lifestyle, anyone can. He acknowledges the reality of the dead not always getting raised, the bills sometimes barely getting paid and healing not always manifesting as we think it should. It is honest and without hype.

Then there is the fact that miracles sometimes happen in spite of faithless prayers. It was this experience that sent Robby on a dive into a Gospel that does what it says it will do. *Do What Jesus Did* is the product. And we are all better for it.

Bill Johnson, senior leader, Bethel Church, Redding, California; author, *When Heaven Invades Earth* and *Hosting the Presence*

1 // Gangsters in the Doorway

Father, make of me a crisis man. Bring those I contact to decision. Let me not be a milepost on a single road; make me a fork, that men must turn one way or another on facing Christ in me.

—Jim Elliot

The door of our church swung open, and in sauntered two of the "princes" from the Latin Kings, the dominant gang in our city. Our church is located in the hub of East Aurora, Illinois, a Latin King hot spot. As they walked in, they simply squared up to me in greeting, hardly twitching a muscle. With a nod to the door, they began pointing out different bullet holes in the building and other scars recalling their past battles. This was a typical "Don't mess with us" threat. When they walked into my church that afternoon, it was because our city was on a brink of an all-out gang war, and they were making it clear that I was definitely in their territory.

Aurora has a long history of violence, from its Al Capone days in the 1930s and '40s to the ever-increasing gang violence of the '80s and '90s, when the gentrifying of Chicago's urban slums squeezed whole neighborhoods of lower-income tenants into our western suburb. The resulting pressure between warring gangs that were being channeled into smaller and smaller overlapping territories often boosted our homicide rate higher than Chicago's. Thanks to exhaustive efforts by community leaders, churches and the police, the situation had finally begun to stabilize. Then the threats began. Outraged by an increasing sense of marginalization and a "lack of respect" from the police, the Latin Kings began issuing warnings that blood would soon flow in the streets. Several drive-by shootings occurred, and a repeat of history seemed imminent.

Alarmed, police began calling me. As a police chaplain I had mediated several high-profile situations in the past and had seen God radically work in the gang community. I currently had several major ex–gang leaders attending my church who had confirmed that a war was on the horizon. After talking with some insiders, I connected with an Aurora businessman committed to community-gang relations. He had grown up in school with one of the major Latin King leaders, and through this connection he often was able to serve as a liaison. He agreed to set up a meeting for me with two of the main leaders. They had street names like Diablo. I had seen their faces on the police station walls for years, and now seeing them framed in the church doorway with nothing but thin air between us sent a quick jolt down my spine.

One gang leader, Shotgun, was in his forties, a fiercely grim-faced man who seemed possessed by an obsession with death. (Shotgun is a nickname I gave him; I've changed some names in my stories to protect people's privacy.) His second man, Diablo, was mainly silent but kept his eyes locked on me the whole time, watching my every move. A woman with them, Diana, had also come. She looked rough when she walked in and was a fiery talker. She had no problem letting me know who she was and what she was about.

I had two of my dear friends with me. Todd White was one, and Darren Wilson was the other. Darren was working on a documentary about the power of God.

Shotgun wasn't too interested in introductions. He was doing most of the talking. In candid detail, he described for us a shoot-out that had occurred on the front property of the church and the killing that took place at the corner of our building. He was letting us know just who it was I was dealing with. Without being too specific, he let us know that "they" were about to do some damage in town. He told me that "some people" in the gangs weren't happy, and if that kept happening, there would be blood in the streets. He said a lot of people were going to get "really jacked up," and added, "If people aren't careful, things are going to get really crazy around here."

I had watched Shotgun before, in the park across the street. One afternoon he and a friend got out of a car and strolled into the crowded park. Within a few minutes, the other men in the park stopped what they were doing, walked over to shake his hand and his friend's, then backed away carefully. The men took their families and left. Women pushed their strollers quickly out of the park, and twenty minutes later there wasn't a sign of life on the block. This was a man who wielded fear in our community.

I looked at Shotgun now and thought about how much God actually loved this person standing before me. I told him squarely, "I know there's the threat of a war, and that can't happen."

The two men looked at each other. "Yeah, is that why you invited us here? To try and stop the war?" Diablo asked.

"No," I said. "Actually, I asked you to come here so that I could introduce you to God."

That was obviously the last thing they expected to come out of my mouth. Diablo looked at me with the strangest expression, then clutched his crucifix and said, "What do you mean? We know who God is!"

I studied him. "Yes, that might be true, but you've never met Him the way you're about to. If you'll let us, we'll pray for you, and you'll meet God." I glanced over at the businessman and asked, "Could we start with you?"

This businessman attends our church now, but at the time I didn't know him well at all. He's a tall, well-built businessman who heads up the Latino business network in the area. He may have been from a mildly Catholic background; I wasn't sure. But whatever his beliefs, clearly the last thing he had expected us to do right then was to pray. He seemed especially surprised to suddenly find himself at the center of it. Thankfully, he agreed to go along with it, though I realized that if this didn't go well, he would probably never meet with me again. I intentionally wanted to start with him because he was the leader of our meeting and the gang leaders trusted him. What he experienced would help legitimize it for the others as he encountered the reality of God and what He was about to do.

We began to pray, "Lord, we bless my friend." I knew he had had an accident years earlier and had suffered back trauma ever since. As we prayed, I recalled this and felt led to pray for healing. The suffering from his back injury was something he struggled with on a daily basis, and his attempts to find ways to numb the pain had negatively affected his life. I asked him if his back still hurt, and he confirmed that he was in pain at the moment from both his back and his shoulder.

I told this man in front of the others, "God is about to make Himself real to you and completely heal your back and take away the pain." We prayed, commanding his back to come into alignment and be fully healed. After a few minutes we asked him to check his back. I could feel God's presence in the room.

He started to move and twist, his eyes widening in disbelief as he realized that not a single twinge of pain or discomfort remained. He said out loud, "It's gone! I can't believe it. It's been years since I've been without any pain." He sat there perplexed. "I don't understand where it went."

His childhood friend, Shotgun, looked at him. "Are you for reals, man?" (Yes, for reals, not for real. For reals is a very typical phrase in poor urban areas; I hear it in my church every week.)

The rest of the meeting the businessman was silent, his face half hidden behind his hands as he seemed in deep thought, considering what had just happened. He told me later that he felt heat and electricity come over his whole body when we prayed for him. During the rest of the meeting, he didn't try to stop us or intervene in anything else we did, although later he told me it was way outside what he felt comfortable with.

Diablo had been leaning forward and staring at me the entire time, rocking back and forth a little in his chair. From experience, I could tell already from a few things that had happened that he actually was demonized, but I could also see a look of great hunger on his face. It seemed as though what had just happened with the businessman had peeled a layer off Diablo's defensive mask. He seemed a little softer and I saw desperation in his eyes, almost like, "I don't know what this is. It scares the hell out of me, but I just have to have it. . . ." His desperation was reaching past the barrier wall—past the dark stronghold of fear and destruction that had defined his life.

We turned to Shotgun and I asked, "Can we pray for you next?" I also asked him if he had a daughter. I sensed the Lord telling me that He wanted to heal Shotgun's relationship with his daughter.

Shotgun answered, "Yeah, I have two daughters. Neither of them will even speak to me anymore."

Then I asked him if something was also going on in his back. I sensed the Lord wanted to heal that, too.

He confirmed, "Yeah, I was shot in the back a while ago; it's still always in pain. One of the disks was permanently messed up."

My friend Todd White, who was sitting next to me, also asked Shotgun if one of his legs was shorter than the other.

"Yeah, that's right." He nodded slowly, as if a bit mystified by what was happening around him.

Todd asked if he could take Shotgun's shorter leg in his hands, and he spoke to it: "Leg, get out here! Bones, muscles, skin, grow right now."

The leg shot out as we watched. Diablo's eyes popped open, and he stood up to check it. Everyone was stunned.

"Yeah, it's straight now," Shotgun confirmed. His back pain was also completely gone.

I looked at him with so much love. "You know, what God just did with your back, He wants to do with your entire life."

The guys looked at each other, and it was as if something had broken in the room. Diablo was next. I sensed God prompting us with a word of healing for his torso area, and Todd said he felt God highlighting Diablo's stomach in particular. Diablo lifted up his shirt and showed us scars where he had been shot in the stomach. A huge chunk was missing where the wound had been. We prayed for the pain to leave and for complete healing to occur in his stomach.

Diablo's eyes widened, and he grabbed his stomach. He said he felt heat and electricity there, and that he had felt it all over him since the moment he first walked in the door.

We explained that what he felt was often a manifestation of God's presence that comes bringing healing. Todd then began praying for Diablo's scarring to disappear. Honestly, we couldn't tell much of a difference afterward, but the two gang leaders swore it had changed and said it was about 50 percent gone. Shocked, they were stunned into silence. Their posture was completely different from when they had come in; the hardened arrogance, cursing and threats that had surrounded their entrance were gone.

When I looked at Diana, the Lord showed me some of the spiritual weight she had been under. I told her, "You've been having demonic visitation at night, hearing voices and having terrible nightmares."

The brassy, outspoken Diana dropped her head down to her chest and started nodding quietly. We also sensed that the Lord wanted to heal her from the stomach trouble and digestive problems bothering her. She confirmed that she was suffering in those areas, too.

I told her, "Diana, God loves you and wants to heal you. We can pray for you, and all those problems can leave right now."

We started praying and commanding the demonic spirits that had been attacking her to leave in the name of Jesus. As we took authority and bound them in the name of Jesus, Diana began sweating profusely. Suddenly she doubled over in her chair as if pushed, and she gasped and let out a huge sigh of air. With that, a heaviness seemed to lift off her, and her face looked different.

We asked her if she had felt something leave, and she nodded. Then we told her, "This needs to be sealed up so that it can't return. The only way that can happen is if you want to accept Christ."

Diana nodded and agreed she would do that.

We looked around the table, and I said, "That goes for all of you. If you want to pray right now and give your life to Christ, He will continue to heal you and set you free in every area of your life."

They all nodded and said yes. I asked them to repeat a prayer giving over their lives to Jesus and making Him their Lord. Shotgun especially, who was standing behind Diana, was almost shouting the prayer, passionately asking God to forgive him for *every* sin he had committed.

All four of them—the businessman, Shotgun, Diablo and Diana—ended up coming back to join our church on Sunday morning. They've also started new relationships with people in the community. Today, Shotgun in particular is a changed man. When I met him before, he was driven by the spirit of death. Whereas before he looked completely angry and hollow eyed, today he glows with laughter and joy. He is the first one to tell jokes and welcome newcomers to our church.

Diana has not missed a Sunday in church since that day and has become an outspoken advocate for Jesus to everyone she knows. She brought her entire family to our church. Shotgun and Diablo brought some other men they met on the street into our church for prayer, and those men also decided to leave their gangs and follow Christ. For weeks afterward, I would get calls from these former Latin King leaders telling me that they kept experiencing the presence of God everywhere they went—when they woke up, in the shower, when they were eating, all the time. One of them told me, "Robby, this is the best stuff in the world." Crying, he called to say, "I don't know why, but when I think about how Jesus has changed me, I can't stop crying. I want the world to know how much Jesus can change people!"

Needless to say, there never was any gang war after our meeting, but both Shotgun and Diablo are still somewhat haunted by their reputations. Every time they show up on a Sunday morning, cop cars begin circling our church. Yet these men continue to praise God, grow in Christ and bring more and more people into relationship with Him. It's interesting how God works.

At the end of our meeting when everyone had accepted Christ, I looked at these guys and said, "What just happened here will change this city." I didn't realize it at the time, but I was giving a prophetic word. This meeting took place at the end of 2011, it has now made national news that there were no homicides in all of Aurora in 2012. That hasn't happened since 1946.[1]

Another twist to this story is that we started the church fifteen years ago in Diana's sister's living room! I remember her sister, Bobbie, asking us back then to pray that Diana would come to Christ and turn away from the life she was leading. Fifteen years later, I had the privilege of leading Diana to Christ when she walked through the door that day. Yet Diana and I did not know our connected history through Bobbie until afterward.

The results of our meeting with the gang leaders became an awesome testimony in our community. It was part of a long series of changes we've seen God bring since we moved to Aurora to plant the church. Many times, it has been an uphill battle. Numerous break-ins have occurred at the church building, and I've had my car stolen several times—twice by members of our church. At different times over the years we've struggled financially, and it has been difficult growing a community of people as committed to the vision as we are. There have been pain and hard times—but in the midst of it all, we've seen incredible breakthroughs time and time again. God has been at work healing, transforming families, restoring marriages, providing jobs and ultimately changing the Aurora community. He has made it a place of hope where people from different parts of the country and even the world come to be trained and equipped.

Interrupted by God

Maybe you, too, have seen incredible breakthrough and transformation right where you are, and like all of us, you long to see such things happen on a more regular basis. Maybe you wonder if it's possible for the "normal" Christian life to look just like Jesus' life did.

Or possibly, you find it hard to relate to the dramatic criminal elements involved in the story I just told. Maybe you wonder why God hasn't answered *your* prayers for healing, yet He does things like healing these gang members instantly. Or you might be asking, "How could this kind of thing apply to the place where I live? To the people I know at my office or at school?"

Maybe you're looking for answers and tools. You're hungry to see the Kingdom of heaven break in to your community. I was just that kind of person when God used me to heal someone for the first time. I was a discouraged youth pastor working in a small, dysfunctional church. I believed God could do miracles in theory, and growing up I had seen things that made me long for more. But the truth was, I was thoroughly turned off by the hype, manipulation and abuse that I had seen in many ministry settings. I knew I wanted to follow God, but I had come to a place of simply hanging in there, resigning myself to a Christian life based primarily on trudging it out and not expecting too much. One of the highest values in the Kingdom of God is faithfulness, but what good is faithfulness without faith? My life was full of church activities and I was faithful to my tasks, but I still had no clue about the authority that is ours to walk in—not for our own sake, but for the sake of the spiritually hungry and for the broken world we live in.

The day that God chose to interrupt me, I wasn't thinking of anyone but myself. I had been hired as a youth pastor, but my vision of ministry had pretty much been brought to its knees by the reality of answering phones and doing the menial tasks that consumed my days. That particular day, I was in a terrible mood. I felt deeply unappreciated by my senior pastor and his family. I felt far from God and from all of the things He had called me to. I was angry and hurt. This was not in any way my shining moment as a Christ follower.

The phone rang, and I answered it halfheartedly. *Probably another sales call*, I thought, *or maybe a message for me to deliver.*

The woman on the phone introduced herself hesitatingly. "Look, I don't really know what to ask," she began. "I don't go to church. As a matter of fact, I'm not even a Christian," she offered apologetically. "I just picked a church from the phone book because my father's going in for heart surgery right now. He's in bad shape, and the doctors say they really don't think he's going to make it. We had to press them to go ahead with the surgery."

She sounded fragile and worn as she explained that this was her father's third bypass surgery, and it most likely meant the end of his life. She didn't know where else to turn, but it had crossed her mind to call a church. She hoped someone would burn a candle, rub some beads for her father, sing a hymn or say a prayer for him in his final stages.

As she tried to rationalize to herself and to me why she had reached out to us, I could tell she was a little embarrassed. Maybe she even regretted that she had bothered to call at all. What could I do? I offered to pray for the surgery with her, though I didn't really want to. It sounded as though her father definitely wasn't going to make it.

"Well . . ." I paused reluctantly, "I could pray for him. . . ."

Frankly, I just wanted to end the phone call as quickly as possible. I didn't think much would change because of my prayer. As I began, it sounded as if I were giving his eulogy: "Lord, just be with this man's family in this difficult time. You're close to the brokenhearted. Help them, comfort them and be near to them in their grieving."

I was pretty much burying the man in my prayers. My thinking was, *Why would God want to heal him? He's not even a believer. God barely even heals any of His own kids.*

Then the Lord spoke something to me that I didn't understand. I didn't hear an audible voice, but I had a strong sense that He was urging me to do something. At the time, I could only point to a few other occasions in my life in which I had heard the Lord speak to me. This was another one. However, I was so distracted by my own concerns that I was almost annoyed at the interruption! What I heard God say was, "Get out on a limb."

What could He mean by that? I wondered.

Then He urged me again: "Take a risk."

I thought, *What am I supposed to do? These people aren't even Christians. There's no risk to take.* Immediately the Scripture came to mind that says, "Open your mouth wide, and I will fill it" (Psalm 81:10 NKJV).

Without really having any idea of what I was about to say next, I told the woman, "I hear God saying He's about to . . ." The words fumbled from my lips, and what I heard coming out was ". . . completely heal your father and give him a brand-new heart, and as a matter of fact, He's going to give him new lungs to go with it."

This was weird! She hadn't said anything about her father's lungs. Have you ever heard yourself say something, then wished you could reach through the air, grab the words and pull them back into your mouth, destroying any evidence that you spoke something so foolish? Most married men know exactly what I mean. As soon as I realized what I had said, I panicked and stopped myself. I began to backpedal as quickly as possible, saying, "Now, wait a minute! What you need to know is that I've never prayed for anyone and seen them healed before. You should know that most of the time when I pray for people, they get sicker, and some have even died. I know that God *can* do things like what I just prayed, but He's never used me to do them. What I just said probably won't happen. . . ."

I was panic-stricken. What if this woman got her hopes up and wound up horribly disappointed? It would be all my fault.

She interrupted me. "You said God is going to give my dad a brand-new heart?"

I gulped out, "Yes, but—"

She cut me off with a brief "Thank you!" and hung up the phone.

With that click of the phone my heart dropped to my toes. What in the world was I thinking? I felt that I had done everything *but* make this woman's pain easier. What if they sued the church? I mean, I was no healer!

When the woman called again crying hours later, my heart sank. I couldn't make out a word she said at first, and I thought, *Oh no, I killed her dad with my prayer. Why did I pray for him? What was I thinking?* I started to apologize profusely: "I am *so* sorry this happened! I am *so* sorry for your loss. . . ."

"What—are—you—talking—about? What—loss?" she stammered.

I could just make out her words through the sobs, and I wasn't sure that I had understood. "Your dad," I said, "he's . . . dead?"

She said, "No—he's doing great!"

Nobody was more surprised to hear that than me.

"Yes, that's right. . . ." She pressed out the story through her tears. "When the doctors opened him up, they said my father had a brand-new heart!" She explained how several years ago her father had had a valve replacement. The doctors had implanted a heart valve from a pig to save his life. All of that was gone. All the scar tissue from the previous surgery was gone. The doctor said it was like the heart of a thirty-year-old man.

I was absolutely stunned. *Could this actually be happening?* I wondered.

She kept going: "I didn't even tell you this, but he had had half his lung removed on that side. You mentioned something about God giving him a new lung. When they looked inside, they also saw that he had a whole lung where they had removed half!"

I kept trying to understand if I was hearing her right. "Are you sure?" I asked. "Now, are you *sure* this happened?" It was hard to wrap my brain around it. God had healed this man, and I could barely believe it. I told her, "I have to see documentation."

Because of my disbelief, she said, "Are you *sure* you're a pastor?" That next Sunday, she came to our church with her whole family. She even brought me her father's medical records from before and after the surgery. Through that experience, her entire family believed God and decided to follow Christ.

For me, it was the breaking in of something I had longed for ever since I was a kid. I saw the reality of God's power and His desire to work through us, which I had been living in complete ignorance of. I hadn't been on some forty-day fast or an in-depth

Scripture study. What I had was a really lousy attitude before she called—nothing seemed particularly holy or superspiritual about that day. Quite the opposite, in fact.

As I thought through this experience, I kept wondering, *Lord, why did You use me to do this? I don't have that ability.*

What I sensed the Lord clearly speaking back to me that day was "Robby, I'm just looking for people who are available."

His Part/Our Part

God's gift to us is ability; our gift to God is availability. He says to us, "You go first. You be available and step out, and I will empower you in the moment." God does His part, and we have a part to play as well. All of us are invited to be part of the unfolding of God's Kingdom reign. It's a high calling and not necessarily a simple journey, but a step-by-step process of faith that's available to everyone, whether you're a brand-new Christian or the pastor of a megachurch.

Do we really believe that the Spirit of the living God lives inside us? What does Galatians 5:16 mean when it says for us to "walk by the Spirit," anyway? It's certainly possible to believe in God without living by His Spirit. Jesus spoke that "God is spirit, and his worshipers must worship in the Spirit and in truth" (John 4:24). By the Spirit we have been given the grace to walk in a level of authority and love that would truly transform the world. One definition of grace that I appreciate is "the power of God, to do the will of God." Living like that is what it means to be Jesus' disciples. It's by the Spirit that we can know Him today, walking with Him and doing the things He did. There is no set standard or comparison of what this has to look like, but there is great encouragement in knowing that God is able to do far more through us than we could ask or imagine (see Ephesians 3:20).

Whether through traditionalism or a multitude of distractions, or through pursuing our own political or economic agendas, somehow the Western Church has fallen asleep to the reality of God's power in our lives. Rather than ministering grace with authority and authentic love, which brings real transformation, we get caught up in rules and judgmentalism. Yet our nation is crying out for hope. Cities are in desperate need of a people of God who genuinely know Christ, who live out and reflect His love. What's needed are not more "Christians," but more Christ followers. There's real authority there—and a freedom that will break through the sickness and suffering and despair of the most impossible situations.

Somehow our "religion" has made it too easy for us to forget the radically inclusive, table-turning, paradigm-shifting Christ of the Bible, and instead, subtly buy in to the lie that Christianity is a little bit boring, a little bit old-fashioned and not quite true in the parts that count.

Nothing could be further from the truth.

2 // First Glimpse

We are not going to move this world by criticism of
it nor conformity to it, but by the combustion within
it of lives ignited by the Spirit of God.

—Vance Havner

The stunning reality of the Kingdom first caught me as a
nine-year-old in Atlanta, Georgia. My parents pastored
a small church, and one night my dad brought home a heroin
addict whom they were trying to help detox. My father was a
rough-and-tumble, self-taught entrepreneur and church planter
who had a wonderful passion for helping the poor. He started
several churches, a nonprofit organization, a Christian commune
and a number of different businesses. One of his dreams was
to start a home for runaway teens and drug addicts. We didn't
have enough money to purchase a separate home, so our home
became that place, for the most part, and the most available
bed was the one next to mine. (This is absolutely *not* recom-
mended in any way.)

This seventeen-year-old runaway had been living in Atlanta after escaping from a home where his father had beaten him every day of his life. Trying to survive on his own, he started taking drugs from people there and ended up an addict who prostituted himself simply for a meal at night. When my dad talked to him about the Lord, he responded that he was desperate for change, and that's how he ended up at our house.

I remember waking up and watching this guy gripped by the D.T.'s (delirium tremens) of heroin. It was a grueling sight. Shaking and sweating and screaming out, he vomited all over the bedroom. I watched my father wrap his arms around this kid from behind just to keep him from hurting himself while going through the shakes. On the third day, which is usually the worst, an incredible thing took place.

It was early Saturday morning, around 6 a.m., just as the light started coming into the room. I woke up and saw this guy leaning against the windowsill, looking intensely out into our backyard. I was startled and scared of him because of the past few days. At the time, I had no context for understanding what I was seeing; I simply knew that it was something very bad. I called out to him, "Hey, are you okay?"

He turned around to look at me, and I saw tears streaming down his face. His T-shirt was wet, and it looked as if he'd been crying for a while. He said, "Robby, it's all gone. . . . Jesus walked into the room this morning, and He just took it all away. The addiction, the pain, the sickness . . . my anger and shame. All of it's gone. It's just all gone!" He dropped his head and began to weep again.

I looked at him; a total change had come over his body. What struck me was his profound peace. There was a sense of rest over him and over the room, which I wouldn't have imagined possible the day before. It was as if his face were glowing. I ran to my parents' bedroom, threw open their door and then burst into tears, totally overcome by what had taken place.

Assuming something terrible had gone on, my dad shouted, "*What happened?* What did he do to you?"

I cried, "No—nothing!" As I got out the story of what had taken place, I sobbed, "That's what I want to see for the rest of my life. I want to see God change people's lives just like that."

That young man grew and ministered in our church, and he went on to have a family. The last I heard, he has a ministry of his own. Truly set free from the bondage and brokenness of his past, he became a powerful force in reaching other people who were trapped in lies about who they were and who didn't know their value or the power of God's love for them.

What I saw happen in that young man that morning—that has become *my* addiction, and it marked the beginning of my lifelong journey. I call it my "first glimpse" because I believe that in that time, God implanted the seed in me of what would grow to become my life passion.

As we all know, this is not an instantaneous process. As I grew older, I went through periods of distraction, rebellion and apathy—as many of us do. I saw some incredible abuses in the Church and some unhealthy dynamics that completely turned me away from movements that emphasized the Holy Spirit. For some years my wounds left me guarded, and I protected myself behind a thick wall of cynicism. At the same time, I battled disillusionment because of the lack of power in my own life and ministry. I knew I somehow needed more of God, and I was hungry to see more of the fullness of His presence. I sensed this power and presence of God was not only possible—it was what He desired us to live in on a daily basis.

In His compassion and faithfulness, Jesus broke through it all. He took both my nine-year-old dream and my discouragement and worked through them, building me up to be a blessing to others. In the pages ahead, I will retrace my own experiences of stepping from the improbable into the impossible. I will also share some key insights I have gained into what it means to follow Jesus in doing the things He did—even through our doubts, through our fears and through our lack of understanding. *We are not disqualified by our doubts.* We're often distracted by our shortcomings and our sense of limitation, but the reality is, it's not about us—it's about Him. From start to finish, it's a story of grace and God's ability to reach far deeper into us and through us than we ever thought possible—to love, to touch, to heal and to demonstrate that His nature is perfect, good and holy.

What I witnessed that day as a nine-year-old is the foundation for what I believe it means to minister as Jesus did. The encounter was so powerful and so simple that even a fearful, wondering little nine-year-old boy was irresistibly drawn in. What I saw in that moment was Christ's love for lost people like us. The guy had no job, no family who loved him, no value of himself—nothing. From the first day I met him, I had watched him vomit up his insides all over my room. Was there hope for him? The world would say no. And yet it was there in my room that Jesus came and appeared to him.

How many of us have spent our whole lives worshiping and going to church three times a week, yet have never seen Jesus? But there He was . . . Jesus . . . in my bedroom, coming down to talk to some guy who didn't even believe in Him or care if He existed. Even as a child I had heard that Christ died for sinners, but somehow the fact that Jesus showed up face-to-face two thousand years later—in the glamourlessness of a little boy's messy bedroom—to talk to a poor, shivering, vomiting kid and to just be with him completely tore me apart. I mean, who was this kid, after all? Who are any of us?

It was love that came into my bedroom that morning. A hippie boy prostitute who had only ever heard his father scream out, "I hate you and I wish you'd never been born!" was gripped by the King of Heaven, who overthrew that message of loathing with His own message of unbridled love. Love set that guy free. Love rescued him from far more than heroin and brought peace and wonder to his face like he had never known. It was love that allowed me to be there, see this guy change before my eyes and realize suddenly, *This is it!*

It's what the prophets prophesied. It's what Israel awaited. It's the longing that escapes in quiet sighs from so many church pews. We know there is more. We yearn for good news that's *really* good. Without realizing it, it was what I had been waiting my whole nine-year-old life to see—and then I knew, in a sudden burst of childish tears, that this was what I wanted to keep seeing for the rest of my life.

This is what the poetry and the power of God's Kingdom is all about. Eight hundred years before Christ, the prophet Isaiah wrote to the insignificant, struggling, almost decimated nation of Israel about something that was coming, *someone* who was coming, who would change everything. In Isaiah 61, he described this man—the Christ—on whom the Spirit of the Lord rested, and who had come to do the following:

> to proclaim good news to the poor.
> . . . to bind up the brokenhearted,
> to proclaim freedom for the captives
> and release from darkness for the prisoners,
> to proclaim the year of the Lord's favor . . .
> to comfort all who mourn,
> and provide for those who grieve in Zion—

> to bestow on them a crown of beauty
>   instead of ashes,
> the oil of joy
>   instead of mourning,
> and a garment of praise
>   instead of a spirit of despair.
>
> Isaiah 61:1–3

Isaiah was writing about the broken, the desperate, the sad, the grieving. He was writing about that seventeen-year-old who went from being a prostitute whom no one wanted to a prince with Christ and an outstanding leader in his community, who ransomed others back to God. God's style of revenge is to rescue the broken and then turn them into rescuers.

In my case, God redeemed the sense of powerlessness and disillusionment I experienced and filled me so that I could become part of fulfilling and equipping others for the incredible move of the Spirit in this generation. This is not for an isolated few. The prophet Joel recorded God's promise about His Spirit working in the last days:

> I will pour out my Spirit upon all people.
> Your sons and daughters will prophesy.
> Your old men will dream dreams,
> and your young men will see visions.
> In those days I will pour out my Spirit
> even on servants—men and women alike.
> And I will cause wonders in the heavens and on the
>   earth.
>
> Joel 2:28–30 NLT

Following God, I've lived stuff straight out of a superheroes movie, except it's real. We serve a creative God who makes the impossible a reality. Living in obedience to Him is the biggest adventure we'll ever have. Life is short, and God wants to give away so much through us. The biggest encouragement to me is seeing countless people from all walks of life accept this challenge of living an adventurous life of risk taking for Him. Young people, old people, rich, poor, homeless, prostitutes, schoolteachers, doctors, gangsters, professional football stars, businessmen, stay-at-home moms—no cookie-cutter mold exists for whom God wants to use or what He is able to do through us if we're willing. When you call on God for breakthrough, you're calling on the beautiful, creative power of God that created the earth in Genesis. But you're also calling on that destructive power of our great warrior King. The very power that we see destroying the kingdom of Satan in the book of Revelation breaks in on our present experience and brings change.

Things are beginning to speed up. All around the world, we're seeing amazing revival. Underground churches in China and Iran overflow with hundreds of thousands of members who are desperately hungry for God despite constant persecution, and who are changing their cities. By the power of God, the dead are being raised all over Africa and in different parts of the world—including the suburbs of the Midwest. New movements of hope are springing up in the ancient places of Egypt. From the urban slums of the Philippines to the gypsy camps of Eastern Europe to the explosion of prayer movements and revival all over Latin America, the Kingdom of God is being declared. The Lord is supernaturally breaking in with power to free people and heal them, bringing them into the reality of His love. When we declare the Good News of the Kingdom, things happen. Blind eyes open, cancer disappears, hearts are made new, crooked legs are straightened, families are reconciled, gang violence stops, Mafia leaders repent, Satanists start preaching Jesus and hope springs up again in the wastelands.

This is what it means to be the Church—not to be perfect, or better than our neighbors. It means that the good news of God's love actually lives inside us and is available to build up, restore, heal and transform the world around us. This is the treasure—the hidden pearl of great price that we seek before anything else. It's the beauty of the Kingdom and the wonder of its King that compels us. We serve a creative God. He never does the same thing the same way twice. This book is not meant to reproduce the Robby Dawkins way of doing things, but to declare that God is on the move and that we can do what Jesus did. Neither is this book a theological exposition, an apologetic or even a comprehensive overview of the topic. It's a training tool to restore the vision, passion and boldness for the Church to rise up and be the Church that Jesus builds. He's not only saving people from sin, but He's saving people *for* victory and glory over the kingdom of darkness, and to bring back the cities to Himself.

My life story is a testimony to that. It is also a testimony to God's reality, His tremendous power and His desire to use us to prophesy over, heal and help restore the mothers, fathers, sons, daughters and communities of this generation to the Father's love. My story is fruit from my life, and I am just one of many with such fruit. God wants every one of His children in every one of His churches around the world to have such fruitful stories.

Even as you're reading this book, I trust that God is stirring your spirit within you and working within your unique combination of gifts and background, your upbringing and even your friends, family and the social circles you belong to. These things are not a coincidence—with God, everything is for a purpose. My aim is to ignite the vision, to encourage you, to empower you and to dare you to step out into the things you were created for since the beginning of time—to pitch you the ball and watch each and every one of you knock it out of the ballpark.

3 // Dry Bones

> The continuous and unembarrassed interchange of
> love and thought between God and the soul of the
> redeemed man is the throbbing heart of New Testa-
> ment religion.
>
> —A. W. Tozer

The Bible is a history of men and women who sought and encountered God's presence. Joseph saw Him through dreams. Esther sought Him through prayer and fasting. Jacob wrestled with Him in the night. Moses waited on a rumbling mountain until God showed him His back. David wrote Him pages of songs and poetry. Mary neglected her chores to sit with Him. Abraham argued with Him. Elijah hid in a cave until he recognized the still, small voice of God. Mary Magdalene washed Jesus' feet with her tears.

As the person God chose to lead His people from slavery to the Promised Land, Moses knew that it was key to be a "People of the Presence." At one point, God was ready to send the Israelites on their way without His presence. He told Moses they could have the Promised Land—with all its wealth, comfort and goodness—but He would not come along. The Lord spoke to Moses, "Get going, you and the people you brought up from the land of Egypt. Go up to the land I swore to give to Abraham, Isaac, and Jacob. . . . Go up to this land that flows with milk and honey." God told them He would send an angel before them, then He added, "but I will not travel among you" (Exodus 33:1–3 NLT).

Basically, God was saying, "You don't want Me; you want My bling, the stuff I give you . . . the rich land flowing with milk and honey. Just go get it." Going to the Promised Land was God's idea. It was His plan for the Israelites, but Moses knew it was never a substitute for God Himself. In the Christian life, it's easy to get caught up in the "bling" of God and get distracted or mistake it for God Himself. His promises for our lives are good, but those promises can never become our sole focus. Whether they involve our marriages, our kids, our work, our ministry or our personal development or success, His promises can easily become our pursuit in many ways—our prayers are filled with requests for wealth, blessing and respect. In the spiritual realm, we can even start desiring the miraculous rather than God's presence, or the bling of a successful ministry or a growing church. If the Holy Spirit left our homes or churches, would anything change? Would we notice? We get so focused on what we see as the end goal that we forget the Lord, from whom all good things come.

Moses saw through that. He knew God's people needed more—the bling was not enough. Moses knew in his heart, *We need God Himself with us, or we are a lost people.* He reminded God of this, and God answered him, "I will personally go with you, Moses, and I will give you rest—everything will be fine for you" (Exodus 33:14 NLT).

Here we see the strength of Moses' leadership, as well as a Kingdom value. Moses could have been satisfied with God's blessing and the presence of God that he himself experienced, but he held out for God's bigger vision, God's original plan of being with all His people. The presence of God wasn't just for a holy few—those who encountered God being the rare exceptions—it was to be the defining characteristic of an entire people and a reflection of the promised kingdom. Though Moses was stranded in the wilderness with no food, no water and thousands of complaining people to look after, he told God, "If you don't personally go with us, don't make us leave this place. . . . For your presence among us sets your people and me apart from all other people on the earth" (verses 15–16 NLT).

The ultimate premium for Moses was the presence of God with His people. Moses didn't view seeking the presence of God as a luxury afforded by the contemplative life once they were more settled, with a house in the burbs, when things were less busy. He was personally responsible for a refugee resettlement project involving over two million people in the desert. None of us have faced the pressures and demands that Moses must have faced in those days. But he left everything and for forty days and forty nights contended for being a "People of the Presence." Moses was desperate for the presence of God.

Going Deeper

Moses also told the Lord, "Let me know your ways" (Exodus 33:13 NLT). Following the ways of God means dependency on Him rather than on our own abilities. When Moses killed the oppressor with his own hands in Egypt, he was more concerned with his own end goal of being "the Liberator." Then he went from being a prince of the most powerful nation on earth to banishment in the desert, where he became the most humble man on earth. His time in that desert was a formative time in which he learned the things he would need to know to lead a people. After forty years, Moses' end goal had matured beyond his personal ambitions, and he had become more concerned with God's purpose and plan for His people. God met him in the desert and said, "Now go, for I am sending you to Pharaoh. You must lead my people Israel out of Egypt" (Exodus 3:10 NLT). Once the Israelites were on their way, God called Moses His favored one, telling him, "I look favorably on you, and I know you by name" (Exodus 33:17 NLT).

Just as with Moses' desert experience, the objective of the desert for the people of God wasn't to take them into the Promised Land. Walking only a couple of miles a day, they could have reached where they were headed in a year. Their time in the desert was formative, too. It familiarized them with God's ways. In the forty years they traveled, God was teaching His people to recognize where He was. The deeper into the desert they went, the more deeply they encountered God.

Moses insisted that God go with them on their journey into the Promised Land and be their God, but he didn't stop at that. He told the Lord, in effect, "Now take me deeper!" Look at his exchange with God:

> The LORD replied to Moses, "I will indeed do what you have asked, for I look favorably on you, and I know you by name."
>
> Moses responded, "Then show me your glorious presence."
>
> The LORD replied, "I will make all my goodness pass before you. . . . For I will show mercy to anyone I choose, and I will

show compassion to anyone I choose. But you may not look directly at my face, for no one may see me and live."

Exodus 33:17–20 NLT

The goal, the objective for Moses, was always God Himself. Moses wasn't satisfied with anything less.

Encountering God's Presence

What God told Moses in their encounter is still true today. When we come into proximity with God and seek His face, parts of us must fall to the side and die. Those parts cannot be near God and live. Faced with His glory, our pride dies, our arrogance dies, our will dies. . . .

That happened in me. Because of some abuse and hurtful situations that I had faced, I backed away from anything I considered charismatic or "weird." Yet at the same time, like Moses, I knew I desperately needed more of God's glory and presence in my life. I was dissatisfied and keenly aware of my shortcomings. I went through an uncomfortable time, but I felt I had found a safe haven as a youth pastor in an older, established church. One Sunday night, a woman from Finland was invited to come and speak. She was a tiny woman, maybe four foot eleven. When she started speaking, I strained forward in my seat to hear her. Her English was almost impossible to understand, and her accent was horrible. I rolled my eyes. *Good grief*, I thought, *why is my pastor wasting our time having her as the main speaker tonight?*

The most I could gather from what she said was that she had gone through a lot of painful experiences and had suffered a lot of depression. Then she described going to a meeting where a man called "Vimber" was preaching. (I didn't know it at the time, but she was referring to John Wimber, founder of the Vineyard

Church Movement, which I am currently part of.) She talked about being at the "Vimber" meeting and getting really drunk. I didn't understand what that meant (other than in the worldly sense), so the more she spoke, the odder she seemed. I couldn't understand why she had come to speak to us.

The woman finished her talk and said, "I pray for people now, ya, ya, ya." She invited people to come up, and people would walk up for prayer and then fall down when she prayed for them.

I had been annoyed at her talk before, but now I was furious. I had seen this type of abuse before! My wife and I had had the best in the business try to get us on the floor. I told Angie, "Let's get out of here."

Angie said, "You can't leave; you're the youth pastor." After a little while, Angie added, "I'm going up for prayer."

"You're crazy!" I said.

She said, "Robby, something's different here. I can feel it. There's something to this."

I said, "This is that same garbage we experienced before."

She said, "I'm going up there."

Then I said, "Actually, you're probably the best person to go because you're going to expose it. You'll get up there and you'll show them, because nobody's going to get Angie down!"

Angie went up and the woman barely touched her before Angie fell over backward on the ground.

My mouth dropped open, and my first thought was, *I wonder what "technique" the woman used to manipulate my wife?* I had seen ministers tip people over by pushing the top of their head or by rocking them with their hands back and forth and then letting go.

After a while Angie got up and came back to where I was sitting. She said, "Robby, this is real. You've got to go up and get prayer."

I said, "This can't be real; you're deceived!"

Angie said, "No, this is real, and you need this."

I went up, still half thinking that my purpose was to expose this woman as a fraud. I was the one who would bring justice to all of this. . . .

The woman looked at me and asked if I wanted prayer. I said, "Yeah, but I'm not closing my eyes." I also put my leg behind me in my football stance to keep me upright. I'm a big man, and even if someone can budge my front leg, there's no way they're getting past the second leg.

The Finnish woman went to pray for me. She reached up to touch my head, but then she drew her hand back before she touched me and said, "No!"

In my head I thought, *That's right, little lady! You realize you can't get one over on me.*

She then waved her hand in front of my face and said, "Fadder, *You* do it."

As she did that, I suddenly realized I was tipping backward in the air. I was shocked. I saw the ceiling spinning past my eyes, and I literally hollered out, "No way!" Just as I said the word *way*, I froze in that position—mouth open, eyes wide in disbelief, hands frozen up by my head like claws, in shock. The guy catching people didn't catch me till I was eighteen inches from the ground. The impact of my weight split his pants from zipper to belt loop. He had to borrow a woman's sweater to tie around his waist for the rest of the evening. I lay frozen for around three hours, tears streaming out of my eyes. I knew something was happening in me, but I didn't know what. I wasn't feeling anything in particular, but I was frozen in place. I remember that the whole time, my eyes were open, and I was thinking, *Why am I crying? Why am I crying?*

Vision of Dry Bones

During that time, I had one vision from Scripture. I was standing in the valley of dry bones described in Ezekiel 37, but it was as if the text were completely gone from my mind and I had never read it before in my life. I was experiencing everything in it for the first time—firsthand. I saw the bones spread out before me in every direction, and as I walked, I saw that they were so dry, so parched, so brittle that when I touched one, it literally turned to powder. The bones weren't just like skeletons; they were actually in severe decay. The Lord spoke to me the same way He did Ezekiel and asked, "Can these bones live?"

I replied, "Absolutely not."

Then He told me, "Prophesy to them."

I began to prophesy to them, and they became muscle and flesh and began to live. I was standing shoulder-to-shoulder with a living army. I knew it was His Church. In the vision, there were people to my left and to my right. As I began to prophesy, they began to do the same thing, almost in the same way. The army had already risen up. I don't remember a thing I was saying to them, but it was something like "Advance." The valley went from being filled with dry bones to all of a sudden being filled with these living people—not just a couple hundred, but thousands upon thousands.

I was shocked by it all. In that encounter, the part that really gripped me was that I began to realize that *I* was part of the valley of dry bones. I realized that I was one of these people whom God was going to minister to. I had been completely shocked by them and was disturbed by the thought that I was counted among them. And God was saying to me, "You've been the most dry."

At the time, I didn't totally understand what was happening, but I became aware of my dry condition. Looking back, I'd say that I was experiencing the love of God, though I didn't really recognize it that way at the time. Still, at that point I had no concept of worthiness. My view of God's relationship with me was sort of master-son. Until that experience with the Finnish lady praying for me, I was oblivious to intimacy with God. I wasn't even sure if what I was experiencing at the time was intimacy. I wondered if God had blasted me. I felt great, but in my mind I didn't realize why that had happened. My devotional life was not the best in those years. I would do devotions more out of duty, like a servant, and also think, *I gotta put in my time and do this, because I'm being paid by the church*. I felt the need to appease God, but that deep intimacy with Him wasn't there.

It was so bizarre when I got up from the floor. I went to speak to my wife and couldn't talk right. Nothing came out intelligibly. I kept trying, but it just got worse. I began to wonder if God had taken away my ability to speak because I had mocked the Finnish lady's accent. We started walking home, and the farther we got from the church, the drunker in the Spirit I became. Suddenly I understood what the speaker had meant by getting really drunk at the "Vimber" meeting! I could barely stay standing, much less walk a straight line. I remember waking up the next day, and it seemed as though the grass were greener, the sky were bluer and finally I could talk again. I felt wonderful. It felt as if my vision had suddenly gone to 40/20.

I wanted everyone to experience that reality. I became unstoppable in evangelism. I started going to the most dangerous parts of town to pray for people, and I saw many of them experience God. Then I noticed that afterward, when we started praying for people in the youth group, they started shaking and being powerfully touched. I realized then that as this Finnish woman had prayed for me, I'd not only had an encounter with God, but I had received something. I began to hear God more clearly. I began to pray for people who weren't Christians, and they began to encounter God. They suddenly knew He was real, and they responded. I had never seen anything like that before, but for me, it was the beginning of a journey toward understanding what it means to be a carrier of His presence.

A Picture of the Presence

During the Feast of Palms just days before His death, Jesus stood up in the midst of Jerusalem and shouted, "Anyone who believes in me may come and drink! For the Scriptures declare, 'Rivers of living water will flow from his heart'" (John 7:38 NLT). In Ezekiel 47, the prophet gave us a vivid portrayal of the river that flows from the temple of God, which is referred to again in Scripture as "a river whose streams make glad the city of God," along whose banks are trees "whose leaves are for the healing of the nations" (Psalm 46:4; Revelation 22:2). The river described is a portrayal of the presence of God that flows from His throne room.

When Jesus calls us the temple of God and promises that streams of living water will flow from those who come to Him (just as He told the woman at the well), I believe He is referring to this same river described both in Ezekiel and Revelation. I believe this represents the living waters of the Spirit of God that dwell within us when Jesus becomes enthroned in our lives.

We see in Ezekiel's description that this is a river with different levels of increasing depth, and that it brings with it abundant life, fruit and healing for the nations. The presence of God is associated with the throne of God and His Kingdom reign. When Jesus told His disciples, "the kingdom of God is within you," I believe He was making another reference to the streams of living water that will flow from our lives (Luke 17:21 KJV). Jesus also told them, "Abide in me, and I in you. . . . He who abides in Me, and I in him, bears much fruit" (John 15:4–5 NKJV).

We are called to be a "People of the Presence," too, and our ability to host God's presence is probably one of the most determinant factors of our Christian life. Before Jesus, David was the mightiest of God's men. He won tremendous victories for God and was described as "a man after God's own heart." What was David's highest passion? What was his greatest desire? It was the presence of God (see Psalm 16:11; 27:8; 105:4). David sought God in the early morning and late at night. He spent hours in worship, seeking the presence of God. It was no coincidence that David was mighty in worship and a mighty warrior in battle. As ruler over Israel, David was specially anointed with priestly oil to receive the Holy Spirit. Because Jesus made it possible, the good news is that what used to be available only to kings and priests is now available to all of us.

Receive the Holy Spirit

When we are born again, the Spirit comes on us and lives inside us to teach us and guide us (see John 14:16–17). It's by the Spirit that we have intimacy with God. We also see references in Scripture to a filling and baptism of the Holy Spirit that came through Christ (see John 7:39). After the resurrection, Jesus appeared to the disciples and said, "'Peace be with you! As the Father has sent me, so I am sending you." Then he breathed on them and said, "Receive the Holy Spirit" (John 20:21–22 NLT). This appears to be an infilling, like the measure of God's Spirit that He poured into us when we were saved.

Yet Jesus also told His disciples, "I am going to send you what my Father has promised; but stay in the city until you have been clothed with power from on high" (Luke 24:49). John the Baptist referred to this promise when he said of Jesus, "I baptize you with water; but someone is coming soon who is greater than I. . . . He will baptize you with the Holy Spirit and with fire" (Luke 3:16 NLT).

Jesus said, "You will receive power when the Holy Spirit comes on you; and you will be my witnesses in Jerusalem, and in all Judea and Samaria, and to the ends of the earth" (Acts 1:8). This passage would indicate a difference from the disciples' previous experience, when Jesus "breathed" on them. This time, the wording suggests being immersed in a baptism of the Spirit. In the Greek, the word used for *power* here is *dunamis*, from which we get our words *dynamite* and *dynamic*. *Dunamis* is also translated as strength, ability, authority and might. That is why these encounters with the Holy Spirit are sometimes called baptisms. When they take place in the book of Acts, we see a dramatic transformation take place in believers as a result. The disciples went from being confused and fearful to being full of boldness, power and the ability to receive and communicate revelation from God.

For me, a series of encounters with God's presence led to increasing breakthroughs in evangelism and in people responding to the Gospel, along with an increase in my confidence and boldness. Gifts of the Spirit come with baptism (see 1 Corinthians 12:4, 8–11), as well as the fruit of the Spirit (see Matthew 7:16; John 15:5, 16; Galatians 5:17–24). If you want to receive more of the Holy Spirit, simply ask the Father. Jesus encourages us,

> Which of you fathers, if your son asks for a fish, will give him a snake instead? Or if he asks for an egg, will give him a scorpion?

If you then, though you are evil, know how to give good gifts to your children, how much more will your Father in heaven give the Holy Spirit to those who ask him!

Luke 11:11–13

Simply pray, "Father, my power is not enough. Come fill me and envelop me with Your Holy Spirit and with fire. Give me the power I need from the Holy Spirit. In Jesus' name, Amen." Then wait for the Spirit to come on you. You may begin to feel a stirring in your chest or stomach. It might feel like heat or tingling (almost like electricity). You may begin to release out of your mouth communication to God in an unknown language. This is the gift of tongues mentioned throughout the New Testament. Continue speaking that out; it stirs power. Many great books have been written on the subject of being filled with the Spirit and speaking in a prayer language, so I won't go into greater detail here. If you want to learn more, however, let me suggest Mario Murillo's *Fresh Fire*[1] and Jack Hayford's *The Beauty of Spiritual Language*.[2]

The Lord wants to be pursued. He searches for men whose hearts are fully devoted to Him so that He can share His secrets with them, share His glorious presence and reveal Himself. Nothing matters like the presence of God. Not position or the applause of men. Not the fame of this world. None of it matters.

God's encounter with Moses on the mountain established the Old Covenant—but with a glimpse of the New Covenant to come. This glimpse was so powerful that Moses left the mountain wearing a veil. The Old Covenant was a veil that was torn away through Christ's work on the cross, when He finally came to establish once and for all a people who would be known for the presence of God. With His presence, God promised, "I will perform miracles that have never been performed anywhere in all the earth or in any nation. And all the people around you will see the power of the LORD—the awesome power I will display for you" (Exodus 34:10 NLT).

Carriers of the Kingdom

Above and beyond anything else about us, we're to be known as a people of God's presence. Looking back in my own life, I believe my encounters with God's presence were instrumental in my being a carrier of the Kingdom, walking in authority and being able to minister the presence of God to other people. Whether praying with staunch atheists at Princeton University, prostitutes in Puerto Rico, witches at Mount Shasta, Russian mob bosses or the guy at the gas station down the street, I have learned to trust that beyond any healing, beyond the accuracy of a prophetic word or the brilliance of any Christian apologetic, it's the presence of God that touches people's hearts and transforms their lives. When I pray for people, first and foremost I ask, "Lord, let Your presence come." I have learned to wait on this presence—to give it room—and to expect that His presence will move mountains of hopelessness, discouragement, anger and unbelief in people's lives.

The authority we carry is in the presence of the Kingdom within us. Many of the stories I have shared in this book are about my journey of stepping out in that reality. As believers, we each have our own stories about the places in which God has pursued us and revealed Himself to us so that we become carriers of the Kingdom. The resurrection power of the cross is within every believer from the moment he or she is "reborn" in the Spirit. The only place the Bible tells us to strive is when we are striving to enter His rest (see Hebrews 4:11). We can rest in knowing that the Kingdom of God is within us, and as we seek first the Kingdom of God and His righteousness, and as we follow, we begin to encounter deeper and deeper levels of His presence.

We are in God's love, and His love is within us. His Kingdom within us is stronger than any atmosphere we'll ever walk into, and the atmosphere of the Kingdom within us is stronger than any circumstance we'll ever encounter. We may not always *feel* that way, but it is a spiritual reality we can act on. Whether we're speaking healing over a person, over a city or over a nation, there is power in our words when we proclaim, "Your Kingdom come, Your will be done on earth as it is in heaven."

4 // The Upside-Down Kingdom

In essentials unity, in non-essentials liberty, in all things charity.

—Marco Antonio de Dominis

In *Crucial Questions about the Kingdom of God*, George Ladd describes the Kingdom of God as "the sovereign rule of God, manifested in the person and work of Christ, creating a people over whom he reigns, and issuing in a realm or realms in which the power of his reign is realized."[1] Because of the human tendency to abuse power, many have backed off from manifestations of God's presence in the Church. They mistrust movements that emphasize moving in the power of the Holy Spirit, yet Jesus walked in power. To call ourselves Christ followers, to seek to do the things that Jesus did, means coming to terms with also walking in His power. The proclamation and demonstration of the Kingdom of God was the central aspect of Christ's ministry of reconciliation. It's not simply a message of words. It's not simply a message of kind acts. Paul said, "My message and my preaching were not with wise and persuasive words, but with a demonstration of the Spirit's power" (1 Corinthians 2:4). God demonstrates His love with powerful acts.

It's important to clarify that when we talk about *power*, we do not mean it in the worldly sense of the word—"power steering, power lifting, power suit" stuff, sort of like an amped-up '80s version of Christianity. That type of power comes with a lot of hype that puts the self at the center and appeals to our pride. Power is there—authentic power—but it can never, ever be separated from the presence and person of Christ (see Ephesians 1:18–20). As Martin Luther often argued, and as Dietrich Bonhoeffer affirmed, "Everything depends upon knowing the person in order to recognize the work."[2] Satan's rule came through exalting himself in pride. Ever since Eden, his appeal to humankind has been to mistrust God's goodness, seize power and exalt themselves to a godlike status. We already were godlike, made in God's image and gifted with authority, yet we fell for the trick of becoming something we already were.

But God is humble. Jesus was God and delivered a death blow to Satan on behalf of humanity by making Himself lower, not higher. My friend Greg Boyd says in the movie *Furious Love*, "How God flexes His muscles is by dying on a cross." In the incarnation we see God—the Almighty King of Kings—coming down humbly in the form and frailty of a man to give it all away. Jesus came and made Himself weak, made Himself vulnerable, made Himself open to rejection, attack and humiliation. This humility even made His friends mad; they wanted Him to use His power to show who He was, rule over Israel and overthrow the empire. Instead, He died on the cross. Love was His weapon of choice, and He expressed His power in humility. He did that so that we could be accepted, built up and encouraged. The power of this love—this sacrifice—was His weapon of mass destruction that broke the stronghold of Satan over us and over the earth. Satan tempted Christ to lord it over all of us—even rightfully so—yet He resisted. In humility He preferred us. He submitted to death and so conquered it, rising again to reign in glory and empower us to live by His Spirit.

The Gospel is the proclaimed restoration of unity with a humble God who not only died to cleanse us from sins but rose again in power to live out His life through us and restore righteousness on the earth. Jesus tells us as His disciples, "Behold, I have given you authority to tread on serpents and scorpions, and over all the power of the enemy, and nothing shall hurt you. Nevertheless, do not rejoice in this, that the spirits are subject to you, but rejoice that your names are written in heaven" (Luke 10:19–20 ESV). It's a message of power and right living given to us in word, sign and deed, but the heart of it is the simplicity of love. This is the gospel of hope, a Kingdom in which beauty and power and righteousness extend from the heart of a servant King. It is a message of love and humility from beginning to end—even as we carry and minister the presence and power of the Almighty God.

Not Just a Salvation Message

The Gospel message the prophets foresaw is not just a salvation message. God proclaims that He came not only to heal, encourage and comfort us, but to draw from the brokenness of humanity a people who "will be called oaks of righteousness, a planting of the LORD for the display of his splendor" (Isaiah 61:3). Isaiah saw this all thousands of years ago—he saw a people who would be called *priests of the Lord* and *ministers of our God*—who would go on to "rebuild the ancient ruins and restore the places long devastated" and to "renew the ruined cities" (Isaiah 61:4; see also verse 6 and 58:12). The Good News of the Kingdom doesn't just stop short with us as individuals. It's also about healing us in relationship to our world, its lands and its peoples. It's about the restoration of families, the building up of communities, the care of our environment, the redemption of cities and the glory of nations to be restored as God's unique expression and celebration of Himself on earth.

This is the promised purpose of God's *shalom* proclaimed from Genesis to Revelation. It's a word of peace that implies not only the absence of war, but the flourishing of peoples, lands and crops—harmony, well-being, health and celebration. The words of the prophet Isaiah almost three thousand years ago were written about you and me. They describe what the world has been crying out for since the beginning of human history. This is the upside-down Kingdom that Christ proclaims in His inaugural address (see Luke 4:16–30). Not only does He accept the outcasts, honor them and call them each by name—but in fact He calls *us* His plan of hope for the world. He came for people. Each person is a unique expression of Christ on earth. He came to call back each culture and tribe of the world, to set you and me free from fear and brokenness and shame, to give us His Spirit and build us up. He came to release us as His "priests and ministers" to renew the ruined cities in all the nations of the earth.

Jesus Loves Prostitutes

I was in Puerto Rico and had taken a few young people with me to do street ministry. We came up to these two prostitutes outside of a hospital emergency room and told them that we were looking for people to pray for. "Do you need prayer for anything?" we asked.

"No, no," they said. "We're good . . . we don't have any problems."

Then a quick thought flashed through my mind and I sensed that it was God's leading in the situation, so I asked one of the women, "Do you have a son? I get the sense that he really needs prayer right now."

She looked at me, taken aback, and nodded. "Yeah, actually, he does—he's the reason we're here. He burned himself really badly, and we're waiting to hear from the doctors." She paused, then added softly, "I'm really afraid they're going to take him away because he was alone while I was 'working.'" She looked depressed and shaken at the thought.

We could see that she was under a staggering weight of guilt and fear. We asked if we could pray for her, and this time she agreed. As we did, the Lord showed us even more details about the situation they were in. These were clearly prophetic words, yet she didn't seem moved or touched. She kept nodding in confirmation that the information God was showing us was accurate, but she seemed numb to everything.

I paused and asked her, "Hey, would you mind looking me in the eyes for a second?" I put my hands on both her shoulders and said, "Jesus loves you. He really loves you."

Something cracked in the air. As she was looking back at me, she burst into tears. I told her that I sensed Satan was fighting hard against her getting the message about how much Jesus loved her and how much He wanted a relationship with her.

At that point her friend muttered, "Oh my God, I'm going to start crying, too!"

I turned to her friend and said, "Hey, would you look at me?"

She stepped back. "No, no, I can't. I can't!" she said. "I'll cry, too." But then she did.

I looked her in the eyes and told her the same thing: "Jesus loves you."

She burst into tears. The two women told us later that it felt as though they were looking into the eyes of love. Now, I know for sure that wasn't me—it wasn't an emotional thing I was personally feeling—it was the Father working through me. It's that connection that we have through Christ that carries His presence and love. The world is dying to hear that message of Christ's love.

In going out to minister to people by doing the things Jesus did, always remember that if you don't feel as though you're getting through, or if you feel that other approaches are failing, look people right in the eyes with the message that Jesus loves them. It seems so simple, but it's extremely powerful. Scripture says that the eyes are the window to the soul (see Matthew 6:22–23). It's the love of Christ looking through us that breaks through the strongholds of Satan, every time. I looked around at our whole team that day outside the hospital, and everyone's eyes were tearing up. We could feel the Father's love among us. It was the breath we longed for. It's not necessarily the prophecy or signs and wonders that break through to someone, although those things often accompany our prayers and can be used to open a heart to the Gospel. Our real weapon against the enemy, however, is God's love.

Love Is a Weapon

In approaching people like these two women, it would have been easy to focus on the outward sin of their lifestyle.

What I've seen is that everywhere, both Christians and non-Christians are held in bondage by guilt and condemnation. Satan is the accuser, and we don't want to stand in agreement with him. His desire is to take the world to hell with him. For instance, Satan wants the message that the world hears from the Church to be "God hates fags!" That's not Good News, yet whenever some protestor stands up waving that kind of sign somewhere, the world is convinced that the Church is more about condemning the lost than about seeing them reconciled to God.

God is in passionate pursuit of us all and desires that we all would be saved (see 1 Timothy 2:1–4). He has made a new and living way for us. Our ministry to others should always agree with God's desire to save the broken and hurting. I've talked to many people who struggle with feeling insecure about hearing from God while ministering. Don't get trapped into focusing on yourself and your inability rather than on His ability. He is able to speak to us. We're His children; we were designed for communication and intimacy with Him. He has given us His Word. I often remind people, "Hey, if you get stuck when you're ministering to someone, you already know the message. When you pray for people, look them in the eyes and tell them, 'Jesus loves you.'" Try it. Watch what happens. The Church has become nonchalant to the power of those words "Jesus loves you." The world is dying to hear them.

For three years, Jesus taught His disciples how to minister from hearts of compassion and mercy. That has to be our approach. We have to constantly check our hearts, especially when facing people who seem to be "enemies" of God. Our impulse can be like that of the disciples, who wanted to call down fire from heaven on Jesus' enemies. This was their approach:

And he sent messengers on ahead, who went into a Samaritan village to get things ready for him; but the people there did not welcome him, because he was heading for Jerusalem. When the disciples James and John saw this, they asked, "Lord, do you want us to call fire down from heaven to destroy them?" But Jesus turned and rebuked them.

Luke 9:52–55

This is not Jesus' approach, nor is it what He came to do here on earth. Our battle is not against flesh and blood—it's not about convincing people that they're bad or should be ashamed of themselves. Our battle is never against people, but against the powers of darkness. Nothing is stronger in disarming the kingdom of darkness than love.

Love is the thing Satan can't stand. Love is the weapon of mass destruction. Satan is the one who heaps shame on us—he's the accuser, and in our approach to people, we should never agree with what the accuser says about them. Satan is the one whispering in people's ears, "God is repulsed by you." God is saying, "I love you—I'm crazy about you! Come home to Me." Sometimes the Church gets this backward and communicates shame or judgment—as if talking about love and acceptance would soft-coat the truth or water it down.

There is a flip side, of course. Some people seem to think love means that everyone and everything is okay and that every circumstance should be accepted just as it is. As a father of six, however, if I saw one of my sons sitting in a snake pit where snakes and scorpions were biting him, I wouldn't smile and say, "Hey, I love you, so I accept where you're at." Love does not mean anything goes.

Love is power and passion that take action to set people free. My experience is that there's nothing soft-coated about love. In fact, it's the greatest weapon of warfare God has given the Church. Simply being more aware of needs around us is the way to start loving others. We're here to serve—to listen, to love, to intercede, to bring a message of reconciliation to people from the heart of the Father. When we're willing to take the risk and step out in the belief that Christ is able to work through us, we begin not only to encounter the presence of the Father, but also the reality of what it means to be reborn in Christ through His Spirit. It's a reality with infinite possibility, and a reality I believe the Father is longing for us to step into.

The Atheist Club President

I was in Seattle, Washington, walking up and down the Ave, right at the base of the University of Washington. It's a global food court of sorts several blocks long that is patronized by students, faculty and area residents. Numerous transients and homeless people also frequent the Ave. I was there with a few students, and we were doing power evangelism on the street. We had already prayed for several people and had seen them healed. We also had some other really great encounters. I walked over to a bus stop, where one couple and another guy were waiting. I said to them, "Hey, is there anything we could pray for you guys about? Do you need healing or anything?"

The guy who was there by himself said, "I'm an atheist and I don't believe in God, but I'll tell you what. I'll let you pray for me if you can answer this question for me: Let's say that I'm a murderer and I like raping little girls, and then I like to murder them. And then I die. Your loving, caring God—what's your God going to tell me?"

I told him, "God loves you and has done everything possible to try to keep you from going to hell—"

"No, no, no," the guy interrupted me. "Let's say I like *torturing* these little girls before I kill them. Now tell me what your God would say to me."

I knew exactly where he was going with this. He was trying to get me to say, "You're going straight to hell, you stinking sinner." I looked at him and started again, "God would tell you that He made a way for you. He tried everything to reach you and turn you from that life to draw you to Himself. . . ." I could tell by then that he really wasn't asking a question; he wanted to make a point. So I said, "Look, I know what you want me to say is, 'You're going to hell.'"

He said, "Yeah, that's right! Because your God isn't loving at all!" And he started ripping into these arguments about how God couldn't possibly be loving, and he was using all these big philosophical words—laying out this whole argument about how God could never be good.

To tell you the truth, I really love apologetics. Debating is one of my favorite things. Like most people who like to debate, I consider myself pretty good at it, and I was completely familiar with the approach this guy was taking. I really felt I could have won an argument with him—in fact, I would have loved to. But I knew that was a trap. Our conversation wasn't about me making a point; it was about reaching this guy and whatever had made him so angry at God. I backed off and instead made myself lower. Atheists have a god they worship called their intellect, and if you'll just tip your hat to it a little, they'll often open up more to you. So I said, "You know, I can see that you're really, really smart—way smarter than I am. I probably couldn't answer all your arguments. But sir, I'm just a simple man, and if you would be so kind as to let me, I would still like to pray for you and bless you."

He gave me a knowing look, as if he were thinking, *Oh, you poor little thing . . . you're kind of stuck, but you just want to pray for me so you can get your little notch on your belt.* He sighed hugely and agreed, "Okay—just make it quick."

By this time, quite a few passersby had stopped to watch. I started praying, "Father, this man is really smart. He's got a lot of questions that I can't answer to his satisfaction, but show him how real You are. Show him how much You love him, how much You care about him and how much You want a relationship with him."

As I prayed, the atheist was muttering, "Uh-huh, uh-huh, yeah, yeah," with sort of a *Hurry up, get it over with—this doesn't touch me at all* attitude. Then he slowly stopped and became quiet.

I sensed then that something real was taking place—a shift had occurred. I asked again, "Father, lavish Your love on him. Show him how real You are and how much You love him. Give him unquestionable proof of Your great love for him."

I finished the prayer, and the guy looked at me. Then he surprised me by dropping his head onto my chest and bursting into tears. Really weeping! What I didn't know at the time was that he was the outspoken leader of an atheist group on campus. He was quite an incendiary speaker and was well-known for his opposition to God. As people in the area realized I was praying for him, a crowd gathered. I hadn't noticed, but by the time we were done praying, about twenty people surrounded our team. As they watched this man experience something profound, many of them actually lifted their hands and said, "I'm next!"

Our team was suddenly swamped with people asking for prayer, and we remained at the bus stop another forty-five minutes, speaking and praying with students. The atheist guy stood there with us, and he didn't stop crying the whole time. I checked back with him, asking, "Are you okay? Do you know now that God loves you? That He's real?"

The guy just nodded; he couldn't even speak for some time. He could only cry and shake his head.

Heads Low, Faith High

A huge temptation exists to step into confrontation when someone challenges us. The world tempts us to use our own power to persuade people—whether it's our God-given intellect, brilliant arguments or sometimes the strength of our personality or charisma. Jesus had all of these things. He amazed people when He taught. But when He was confronted, He resisted temptation and trusted the Father. He was often silent, or He asked good questions. Sometimes God will work through a word of wisdom or knowledge or give us a clear understanding about the way we can best answer people. In this situation with the president of the atheist club, I knew it was simply a matter of pointing to the reality of God's love for him through prayer.

We need to lay down our need to defend or prove ourselves, and instead look to the Father for direction. Spirit-led evangelism forces us into a place of dependency on God to do the impossible, even working through us. Our boldness comes not from confidence in ourselves, but from believing Him and declaring the things that only He is capable of fulfilling.

Sometimes in the moment, prayer or love can *feel* like a weak solution. We treat it like the truce flag, as if we've reached the end and have to give up when we say, "We'll pray for you." It can be tempting to try to find an alternative to that feeling of weakness or exposure, but there are times when that's what we're called to be, and there's power in that. When we're challenged by intellectuals, often we're tempted to rise into debate, but I've learned to go low and remember what Psalm 76:10 (NLT) says: "Human defiance only enhances your glory, for you use it as a weapon." I've learned to freely acknowledge, "Wow, I can see you're really smart. You're probably smarter than I am," and then keep it simple. The message of the Good News is often no more and no less than the reality that "God is here." As Luke 17:21 (NLT) tells us, "You won't be able to say, 'Here it is!' or 'It's over there!' For the Kingdom of God is already among you."

When we've reached the end, that's where God steps in. We can trust that. We can even seize that moment of risk. Sometimes this exposes us to rejection, frustration and feeling foolish. Don't worry about it. When the breakthroughs happen, they're incredible. If God deems people worthy of Christ pouring out His life on their behalf, they're certainly worthy of us pouring out our lives. We're not to crush others or proclaim ourselves or try to be anybody; we're to lovingly and faithfully follow in the footsteps of the humble yet Almighty King who goes before us and leads us with His love.

Jesus was always using His power to draw people to a deeper connection with the presence of God. As followers of Christ, our rest, our strength, our comfort and everything we need is in His presence. It's Him we seek. We're to be a people of His presence and walk in His power to carry out His ministry of reconciliation in the world.

Following Jesus also brings with it persecution and rejection. This is not about my blessing, my healing or my comfort, but about glorifying Jesus just as He glorified the Father, and about blessing those He came to die for. I believe the throne of God on this earth was the cross of Christ. The cross is how Jesus reversed the curse that Adam and Eve brought on us all in the

Garden of Eden, which continues to this day. By dying on the cross, Jesus was lifted up and glorified by the Father, and He provided us with a way to come back into right relationship with the Father.

Mark 16:17 (NLT) tells us, "These miraculous signs will accompany those who believe: They will cast out demons in my name, and they will speak in new languages." As we go out as His disciples and declare the Kingdom of God, He accompanies our words with signs and wonders. Healing is a part of how we continue Jesus' work on earth—to destroy the works of the evil one (see 1 John 3:8).

The Kingdom of God is not about our own prosperity, yet God graciously grants us blessing upon blessing—but that is His nature, not our pursuit. We're told to "seek first His kingdom and His righteousness" (Matthew 6:33). Our goal is to know God and walk with Him, doing the things He did, proclaiming and demonstrating the Kingdom of God through His love and reconciling people back to right relationship with Him. As we work with Him, we learn about His heart and His nature. God's pursuit of us originated in the Garden of Eden. As soon as Adam and Eve fell, He knew it. He sees everything. Yet He still came in pursuit to bring us back to that place where we would have intimacy with Him.

Kindness Leads to Repentance

Paul reminds us in Romans 2:4 that it's the *kindness* of God that leads us to repentance, and he reminds us about the incredible "riches of His kindness, forbearance and patience." There's a richness and luxury of love in Christ's ministry. Sometimes we act as if there's a poverty of love—as if there's hardly enough to go around for us Christians, much less for some sinner. Nothing could be further from the truth.

Where we expected judgment in our lives, Jesus came in mercy. Again, it's the upside-down Kingdom where things work the opposite of the way we'd expect. Every little incident of kindness in our lives has been Jesus showing us how much He loves us. God pursues us in loving-kindness. We falsely contrast the justice of God with His mercy, but God's justice is actually described as that which would neither break a bruised reed nor snuff out even a smoldering wick (see Isaiah 42:3). That means God handles us with great care and concern, not with raging, angry judgment. The justice of God and His mercy are one and the same in Christ. His justice is His greatest mercy—it's both perfect and unspeakably gentle. God came to earth not to punish, but to forgive.

We think we are punished until we repent, but in another upside-down twist, we are actually lavished with love until we turn back toward God. When we claim Him as our Father, it's then that God disciplines us in love, never in anger. He creates protection around our lives because He loves us. He brings order so that we can flourish in freedom and peace. He knows our hurts, and He is slow to anger and quick to show mercy. He is always in favor of our advancement, teaching and growth. In every portrait of Old Testament judgment, God wept over every judgment and then restored and blessed those whom He "rejected."

Jesus Loves Witches

An encounter I had with a witch one day clearly illustrated the truth to me that Jesus loves witches. I was with some friends of mine, Darren Wilson and Chris Overstreet. Darren makes incredible documentary films of God stories around the world. He was filming his second movie, *Furious Love*, and asked me to accompany them to pray for people at one of the largest psychic/New Age festivals in the country, held at Mount Shasta, California. I went along, anxious to see what God would do.

We set up two booths inside a large gymnasium at the festival, and we planned to offer prayer ministry, particularly asking God for words of knowledge, healing and deliverance. Using the language of that community, we put up signs offering "Free Readings and Cleansings." Although we didn't hide the fact that we were Christians at a New Age fair, a long line soon formed at our booths for prayer. The first person in my line seemed to anticipate a fight. She brazenly looked at me and the big cross on my shirt and said, "I'm a witch."

I believed her. She was dressed in layers upon layers of black, with sleeves kind of coming to dripping points. There was a big pentagram on her chest. I smiled and asked her, "Would you like for me to pray for you?"

She sort of raised her eyebrows and repeated, "But I'm a witch."

"I would love to pray for you," I told her.

She looked at me, puzzled this time. "You're not afraid?"

I had to smile again. "No."

She asked me again, "You're not afraid at all?"

"No, no," I told her. "I love to pray for witches. As a matter of fact, I've been asking the Lord to send some witches my way so I could pray for them."

She let me pray for her. I prayed simply, asking, "Father, love her, lavish Your love over her. Show her the reality of how much You love her and care for her."

Right about then, I felt this slight pain between my shoulder blades. I sensed that it wasn't a natural pain, but a sympathy pain—like a prophetic manifestation in my body of something that was going on with her. (I'll explain more about this kind of pain in chapter 6, where I cover several ways in which God speaks to us.) I asked her, "By any chance, do you have bad back pain?"

"Yes," she said.

I got another impression from the Spirit and asked her, "Was it from a car accident two years ago?"

She said, "Yeah, it was two and a half years ago. I was in a bad car accident."

I asked her if she had had pain ever since, and she said, "Yes, I've been through three surgeries, but they can't fix it."

My experience has been that whenever God highlights someone's pain to me, it's because He wants to heal it right then, so I told her, "I'm going to pray for your back, and God's going to completely heal it to show you how much He loves you."

I start praying for her and began to command her back to come into alignment. I commanded the damaged discs to be restored and all the pain to leave immediately so that she would know that God loved her and wanted a relationship with her. As I was praying, all of a sudden she sort of lunged forward and started twisting all around. She sounded like a bag of potato chips being crunched around. It hurt me just to hear it.

I asked, "Excuse me, are you okay?" What was happening looked like a strange battle to me, and I wasn't sure if it was good or bad.

She stood up really straight and with total shock gasped, "It's gone!"

I thought I knew what she was talking about, but I wanted her to acknowledge and profess it clearly, so I asked her, "What's gone?"

She said, "All the pain—it's all *gone*." She turned to look at me really sharply as a tear came down her cheek. "Why would God want to heal a witch?" she asked.

"He sees you as someone He loves very much," I told her. "He knows you and loves you."

"But I'm a witch . . . I'm a witch," she kept repeating. It was as though she couldn't accept that God would heal her.

At that point I kind of checked her. "You know, you're starting to sound like Christians right now who don't understand God's love," I said. "The truth is that this healing is from God, who is showing you how much He loves you. He doesn't see you as a witch, but as someone He is inviting to have a relationship with Him."

Suddenly she seemed to see her surroundings with new eyes. "I've got to get out of here!" she exclaimed. "I need to *leave* right now. This is a bad place!" (speaking of the psychic fair). There were big side doors in the conference room, and she pushed her way through them. She had a big booth a few stalls over filled with pentagrams and crystals for sale, but she abandoned everything and never came back. People were walking by her booth and looking at her stuff, and then walking on because no one was there to attend to it.

He Came to Save

Wherever Jesus went, both murmurers and believers were present in the crowds surrounding Him. Many believed, and many didn't. Many condemned Him, and many were offended by what He did and by whom He spent His time with. As we live out our lives, we run across the same kinds of people. We can respond to them either from the critical view or mercy view.

With every person I meet, the temptation is always there to see them from a worldly or critical point of view. The question I always need to be asking is, "Father, how do *You* see this person? Jesus, You're standing right here with us. What are You saying to this one whom You love?"

Christ in us gives us the freedom to act like and to be Jesus to people. Working through us, He reconciles them to the Father, perhaps through healing, words of knowledge or encounters with His presence. Christ came to proclaim the Father's love and to reconcile all peoples to Himself. "I did not come to judge the world," He said, "but to save the world" (John 12:47).

5 // Nickels in God's Pocket

The eyes of the Lord search back and forth across the whole earth, looking for people whose hearts are perfect toward him, so that he can show his great power in helping them.

2 Chronicles 16:9 TLB

And then I heard the voice of the Master: "Whom shall I send? Who will go for us?" I spoke up, "I'll go. Send me!"

Isaiah 6:8 MESSAGE

As she left a conference in Atlanta, Georgia, a woman was praying, "Lord, I'll do anything for You. I'll do *anything*. Just tell me what You want me to do, and I'll do it." In that moment she sensed something and realized, *I'm supposed to turn left.* It almost felt like a whim, but desperately wanting to obey God's voice, the woman turned left. After driving for a little while, she felt as though she was supposed to turn right, so she did. Filled with anticipation, she wondered, *Is God actually directing me to go do something right now? This is so exciting!*

Before she knew it the woman ended up right in front of a little convenience store, which she sensed was the place the Lord was bringing her. Once inside, she couldn't wait to see how the Lord would direct her, but the only thing that kept coming to her mind was, *Go over in front of the clerk and stand on your head.*

Pretty weird, right? How many of us would reach that point and say, "Okay, no, that's not God," and get in our car and drive home? The direction this woman was sensing seemed odd enough that she could have easily discounted it, although it wasn't something immoral or unbiblical. She prayed, "Lord, are You sure?" Then she felt nothing, no confirmation.

So many times, that's the gentleness of the Holy Spirit. He doesn't force us to do anything. He's not a bully, and He won't shove us into doing what we're unwilling to do. In that moment, this woman had a real choice to make. She said, "Okay."

It took her a little bit to build up the courage, and she hung around reading chip packages until everybody cleared out of the store. Then she ran up to the register and said, "Hey! Look what I can do!" There happened to be a pole right in front of the clerk, so she did a handstand against it. From her upside-down position, she saw him drop his head and shake it. She swung her legs down and thought, *Man, he thinks I'm crazy—a real freak!* But she walked up to the register and saw that the clerk was actually crying, so she asked, "What's the matter?"

He told her, "About half an hour ago, I was sitting here working, and I prayed, 'God, if You're real, have somebody come in here and stand on their head.'" The clerk ended up giving his life to Christ as a result of this woman's obedience to God's voice, and he has attended the same church as she does ever since.

This is an unusual story, but I love it because it exemplifies obedience. We may not have too many stories like this to tell, but when we look back over our lives, we often can recognize moments when we sensed a tiny nudge to step out and take a risk. It's so easy to brush off those nudges and tell ourselves, *Nah, that couldn't be God.* Then we continue on our way, attending to the next ten things on our agenda and missing out on God-given opportunities.

Think about what would have happened if this woman had been mistaken in what she was sensing. What would've been lost? Absolutely nothing. Sure, in such situations a little of our dignity is at stake, and maybe a little pride. If you're like me, though, you have some of those to spare. Those things grow back pretty quickly anyway!

More to the point, think about what this woman would've let slip by if she had just walked away from her nudge. Jesus tells us, "Only those who throw away their lives for my sake and for the sake of the Good News will ever know what it means to really live" (Mark 8:35 TLB). The treasure is in the risk. We are willing to die for Jesus, but are we willing to look foolish for Him?

Interrupted and Available

For God to use you, you have to be willing to be interrupted and available. Remember my story in chapter 1 about the woman who called the church and asked for prayer for her sick father? I learned years ago from that situation that God isn't necessarily looking for qualified people; He's looking for *available* people whom He can use. For instance, one day Jesus and His followers were leaving Jericho when a blind man named Bartimaeus began to cry out, "Jesus, Son of David, have mercy on me." The

Scripture says that Jesus stopped and turned to him, and then He healed him (see Mark 10:46–52). This tells us that Jesus was willing to be interrupted. Doing the stuff of the Kingdom means living by an "as you go" model. Yes, we need to be intentional about being evangelists, but we also need to be "naturally supernatural" people. This requires a willingness to be interrupted.

God isn't always going to grab us by the collar and make us pray for someone or tell someone something for Him. He wants us to *desire* to step into the Kingdom work. Sometimes working for the Kingdom starts as a discipline in us, but it needs to become a passion. If we never become a people of desire, we will never accurately represent Christ on this earth.

Our desires also need to sync up with His desires. When we spend time with God, we start to recognize all the ways Jesus is at work around us, and then we can join in with what He's doing. He knew that the woman in Atlanta desired in her heart to be used by Him. She faced the major obstacle of fear, but she overcame it and made herself available. She had never done anything in her life like what happened that day—telling God she would do anything, then standing on her hands in front of a store clerk—yet she prayed that awesome prayer and let God interrupt her life for His purposes.

I try to pray a similar prayer every morning as I'm brushing my teeth: "Help me pay attention to all the ways You're working around me, Lord, and join in with what You're doing." My confidence builds as I persistently pray, and I can respond to opportunities that come up.

It's easy to lose your nerve or second-guess yourself at the last minute instead of stepping into an opportunity for God to work. The Holy Spirit's voice was described in 1 Kings 19:12 as "a still small voice" (NKJV). His promptings are often light as a feather that lands on your arm; it would be easy to brush it off and ignore it. Sometimes when we first step into a situation, we don't get it right away, or what God's doing is not obvious. I'm sure that when Jesus was talking to the woman at the well, there were some moments where it felt awkward. It took her a few minutes to process what she was experiencing, and at several points the conversation could have turned into a religious argument, yet He stayed with it.

The Father helps us have His heart for people and His eyes to see the world. He will teach us to respond to His voice and to fine-tune our hearing. If we take the risk and go for something 100 percent of the time, we'll probably get it right about 80 percent of the time, yet we need to pursue God encounters like a hunter pursues its prey. When we truly encounter God's presence, other things that once seemed significant just fade away.

In the first chapter, I said that God's gift to you is ability and your gift to God is availability, and that He tells us, "You go first." John Wimber, whom God greatly used in healings and prophetic gifts, said it another way: "God says, 'You go and I'll show.'" Sometimes we forget that. We fail to recognize that our daily life is filled with opportunities for taking risks—for stepping out and trusting that God is with us and is more than able to meet the needs of the people around us, through us. When Jesus faced the hungry crowds, He turned to His disciples and said, "*You* feed them." He was training them to step out in obedience, to step out in risk taking. And as they stepped out, God provided.

Years ago, when I was first beginning to step out in prophetic evangelism, I went to the music store to buy drumsticks for the church. I was in a huge hurry and needed to purchase them quickly and get back. However, I noticed this guy playing keyboards in the corner of the store. He sported a really rock'n'roll look, with cool hair and sunglasses. I walked toward him, but then I second-guessed myself and started to leave. I felt as if I should say something to him, however, so although I had bought the drumsticks and was ready to go, I walked back to him and stood there listening to him play. I realized God wanted to say something to him, but I had no clue what. He was an incredible keyboardist, so I said, "Man, you're really mean on those keyboards."

He lifted his head but didn't respond, acting sort of like, "I know I'm really good."

Then I said, "Hey, do you have a minute? Sometimes the Lord speaks to me about people, and I feel as though there's something God wants you to know."

Even then, I still had no clue what God wanted to say to him. For me, it's often the case that I sense God wants to speak, but I have no clue what He wants to say until I begin speaking. Who knows? This may be God's way of continually keeping me in a place of taking risks even as I encourage others to do so. Some people refer to what happens to me as a prophetic style called "automatic speech" or "automatic mouth." It doesn't mean I don't have control or am not still responsible for what I say, of course.

This guy continued playing, but said, "What is it?"

Without having any idea what I would say, I started out, "The Lord wants you to know . . ." And then the words I felt come were ". . . that He didn't do this to you. It was the result of sin in the world. The Bible says that the price of sin is death, but the gift of God is eternal life. His desire is for everyone to have eternal life, and He wants you to know that He didn't do this to you."

He turned his head away from me for a second, and as he looked back, a tear slid down from under his sunglasses. He asked slowly, "Do you know who I am? Did anyone tell you anything about me?" He paused. "Not that anyone here would know me."

I shook my head, "No, I don't know who you are." I could feel his eyes staring at me through his shades.

"*Nobody* told you anything about me?" he asked again. His chin started quivering, and a few more tears rolled down from under his sunglasses. He told me, "Six months ago, my father died in his sleep. They did an autopsy, and they couldn't find any reason for his death. Then two months later, the night before my fiancée and I were supposed to get married, she died in her sleep. I was called at three in the morning the day of my wedding and was told my fiancée had died. And what you're telling me, what you're saying, is that God didn't do this. I thought God hated me and took my father and then my fiancée the night before my wedding."

I said, "No, the Lord loves you! His gift is life, and He doesn't want anybody to die. It's a result of sin in the world."

He looked at me in silence, then asked, "There's no way that anybody told you all that? Who are you?"

I said, "I'm a youth pastor at a church here in town." He invited me to come and meet with his band and his friends that same night.

The Ultimate Evangelist

The Holy Spirit is a confident evangelist, even when you and I are not. Sometime if you just have a sense that God wants to say something to someone, I would encourage you to step into that in faith. You don't have to consider yourself a prophet or an evangelist; when you have the sense that God wants to reach someone, He will use you to do it.

Second Chronicles 16:9 (NKJV) describes how "the eyes of the LORD run to and fro throughout the whole earth, to show Himself strong on behalf of those whose heart is loyal to Him." You don't have to feel confident in yourself or your ability. God gives grace to the humble. One definition of grace is "the power of God to do the will of God" (see Philippians 2:13). I walked into that situation in the music store completely blind, not having anything in particular to say to someone, but trusting that God did. I was acting in faith when I spoke out, "The Lord wants you to know . . ." Another way to approach this is to look at someone and say, "When I look at you, I see . . ." and then trust God to fill in what He sees about that person.

Many of us expect that the Holy Spirit will sort of apprehend us in such situations, as if He'll come with a megaphone inside our heads or take possession of our bodies and start moving our arms and legs like a science fiction movie character. We think that's what God will do if He wants to use us, but that's not at all what it's like. When we approach people, God wants us to go as ourselves and be ourselves. You might not feel extremely confident in what your spiritual gifts are or operate at a high level of what you think of as "supernatural" ministry. You might not even be comfortable with the idea of evangelism, but the Holy Spirit is comfortable with it. The Holy Spirit is the ultimate evangelist, constantly pointing people to Jesus. As we step out in dependence on Him and follow those small promptings, He teaches us how to reach people.

At the same time, as we reach out to people, we discover more of who God is and we often see an increase of the Holy Spirit in our lives. In advancing the Kingdom of God, we often encounter the King Himself on the front lines. Stepping out and saying "God is here now and wants to speak" is a proclamation of the Good News. It brings with it an expectation that

God will demonstrate His love, healing, freedom and presence to people.

Any Time, Any Place

As Christians, we're often in danger of becoming theoreticians rather than practitioners of the Kingdom. God hasn't called us to be theoreticians alone; He wants us to both understand Kingdom theory and put it into practice. "The kingdom of heaven has been forcefully advancing, and forceful men lay hold of it" (Matthew 11:12 NIV1984).

Paul emphasized that his "teaching and message were not delivered with skillful words of human wisdom, but with convincing proof of the power of God's Spirit" (1 Corinthians 2:4 GNT). This is where the rubber meets the road, and where the Kingdom breaks in. When planting my church in a poor urban area of Chicago, or when ministering near the University of Washington campus in Seattle, I knew that persuasive words wouldn't cut it. A slick presentation alone wouldn't cut it. We needed a demonstration of God's power so people could see that God is real and is pursuing them.

It's wonderful to see how the power of God makes Him tangible to people. It's wonderful to see that moment when the lightbulb clicks on and people realize, "This is real!" It's not about the miracles; it's not about the healing. The goodness and beauty of the Kingdom is about the King. The Kingdom of God is about the revelation of its King and the reconciliation of the King with His people.

I was in Boise, Idaho, with my friend Tri Robinson, who pastors a great Vineyard church in the area.[1] On the way to lunch, we passed by a homeless woman who had this big sign that said, "Diabetic. Need Medication." She was asking for money. I stopped and asked gently, "Are you really a diabetic?"

She squinted at me, "Yeah, I am."

I asked, "Would you mind if we prayed for your healing?" I was actually in Boise to teach on how to pray for people for healing, and Tri was looking at the guys with us like, *Robby's going to do it right now—this is live in action!*

As we prayed, I immediately sensed that I should pray for a circulation problem in the woman's legs and feet. (I found out later that this problem is typical in diabetics.) She told me that yes, her legs and feet were very painful at that moment. As we prayed, all the pain left. There was no way to check her diabetes at that time, but I felt as though the Lord was impressing on me "migraine headaches." I asked her, "By chance do you struggle with migraine headaches?"

She looked up at me strangely and said, "Nooo . . . no, I don't." She stared at me blankly for a few minutes, as if she was processing something. It felt like one of those awkward moments I said can happen, but then she told us, "My husband has terrible migraines. As a matter of fact, he has one now and went to find a dark alley somewhere to lie down and sleep it off."

My heart went out to this guy who was living on the streets, with nowhere to find comfort from his migraines and nowhere to get away from the noise and light to rest. I prayed, "Father, in the name of Jesus we call that husband back here so we can pray for him and break the power of this migraine off his body." A minute or two later, a man walked up to us. It was her husband. She told him that we had asked if we could pray for her diabetes.

The man looked around at us and said, "I was walking down the street, looking for a place to hide and to sleep off this migraine, and a woman says to me, 'You need to stop right now. There's an angel with your wife, and it's going to release healing for you from these migraines.' Then I came back here and found you guys." The man's eyes welled up with tears, and he said, "This is really real."

As I prayed along with Tri and the other guys, immediately the pressure and blinding effect of the migraine left the man. He and his wife were blown away. He had been angry at God for years because of his struggles, but now he felt as though God saw him and heard him.

Tri's church runs a huge homeless outreach in their community, so Tri arranged for this couple to come to his clinic, get her diabetes checked out and get vouchers for any medication she might need. Then he asked them, "Are you hungry? We're just about to eat, and we'd love to buy you lunch in the restaurant so you can enjoy a date together." They took him up on it, and they came to the clinic a few days later. The woman's blood sugar was almost normal, even though she had an extreme case of diabetes and had been out of insulin for days. I believe what God did for the couple that day was huge. As we step out, He steps in.

Push the Limit

All of us have more authority than we realize, and so much more than we currently operate in. The more I've stepped out in this journey, the more incredible things I've seen God do. It has been a process, and often I've prayed for people eight or ten times before I've seen a change. As I've pressed in, however, I've yet to see the limit.

I want to encourage you to push the limit. We know that we're all called to be on a mission exactly where God has planted us, but it's often easy to find ourselves more invested in preserving the status quo—not realizing that this world's status quo is actually at odds with the Kingdom of God and the transformation He wants to bring. We're all descendants of Adam, and he represented the status quo of what was normal and possible for humankind before the Fall. Then came the Fall and all its consequences, but God wanted more for us. When Jesus came, He broke the pattern of sin and paid the price for our freedom. His resurrection means that by the same power, we can live by a new pattern, a new standard. Jesus came as the new normal (see 1 Corinthians 15:45–49).

Living in the Kingdom is living in the gap between the "here" and the "not yet." No matter what level of faith you're living at, it's still a risk-taking lifestyle. Taking risks is the very definition of living by faith; we live not by our past experiences or by what we see, but by what we believe and what God's Word says is true about us—that we'll actually do what Jesus did.

One of the biggest reasons we fail to step into Jesus' transferable ministry is that we mistakenly believe we have to be the source for God's miracles. That thinking not only scares most of us away from praying for others in faith, but it's also bad theory and bad theology. The healing and all the other stuff is God's part to do. I'm just supposed to go. I'm just supposed to show up and respond to what He says to do. I succeed because I've obeyed.

Sometimes we feel as if we have to do things a certain way, and our preconceived notions of how God will use us can get in the way. A girl who started coming to our church had been told by many people over a long period of time that she had a strong prophetic gifting. She believed it, but she waited around for years, thinking that one day words from God would just start shooting out of her mouth. It was a big revelation to her that God uses us to speak to other people in the same way He speaks to us—sometimes in the most natural ways. Pictures or flashes or impressions may come to mind as we pray. It can be through our bodies, which might involve sympathy pain, unexpected emotions (tears, joy or peace) or a sense of peace in difficulties. It even can be through movies that we watch. We worry that what we're sensing is just our imagination, but who said God can't use our imagination? He invented it. He's a creative and imaginative God. It's a huge part of how we are like Him and how we connect with Him.

We shouldn't wait around expecting that God will change us into someone we're not before He uses us. We have a tendency to say, "God, if You'll anoint me, I'll go." God says, "If you'll go, I'll anoint you." His plan is to use who we already are—the same people He made us in the first place, with the same personalities, giftings and weaknesses. Just be *you*. God wants to work through you and me. We aren't the main act—God is. But He's made us a crucial part of the breaking in of His Kingdom.

It Pays to Persevere

As followers of Jesus, we can rely on fairly simple words and actions. God is present, and He wants to do something. It's that simple. How do I know God is present? Because I'm here, and He's in me. As I said earlier, God is looking for people who are willing to be interrupted and available. I'm willing, and I'm coming into a situation in the name of the Lord. I'm not coming in my name or in my power—I'm trusting that because I've shown up, God has shown up.

Jesus says, "As the Father has sent me, I also send you" (John 20:21 NKJV). It's simple how this happens. Luke chapter 10 talks about how Jesus sent out 72 of His followers on a short mission, and they returned with joy, saying, "Lord, even the demons submit to us in your name" (verse 17). He told them to drive out demons and they did, then they were shocked that this promise was fulfilled. The supernatural power of God showed up with these 72 because they *went*. As they acted in obedience, healing and deliverance came, and the Holy Spirit kicked in.

My church is filled with people brought to Christ by the reality of God breaking in to their lives through people like you and me. In our youth group a couple of years back, these giggly, boy-crazy high school girls got saved. For fun, they would hang out in the medicine aisle of Walmart and pray for sick people there to get healed.

Another young man brought his friend Jim to youth group. Jim was a Jewish atheist, and both his parents were atheists. He was sitting at the back of the group, laughing at my kids and others during worship. During prayer time, my oldest son, Judah, and his brother Micah (15 and 13 at the time) asked this young atheist if they could pray for him.

Jim replied, "I'm an atheist. You'd just be wasting your time."

My sons said, "If you're an atheist, you've got nothing to lose if we pray for you, right?"

Jim said, "I suppose you're right. Go ahead, if you really want to waste your time."

My boys started praying for him. They asked that he would be blessed and would feel God's love. In the middle of their prayer, Jim looked up in shock and said, "I hear you!"

My boys thought he was speaking figuratively and responded with, "Yeah, man, we hear you, too."

Jim said, "No, you don't get it—I've been deaf in this ear all my life. I've had five surgeries, and it could never be repaired. But when you guys were praying, it just popped and opened right up instantly."

Jim became an usher in our church. I baptized him and his mother on the same day. For years, Jim walked about three miles to church every Sunday and three miles home, even in the Chicago winters. You could set your watch by Jim. The biggest atheist in West Aurora High School became a great evangelist there. Nothing my sons could say would have made a difference, but God healed Jim's ear and all his doubts vanished in one *pop*. There's no such thing as a Happy Meal–sized work of the Holy Spirit. He does things in a supersized way.

In Romans 6:13, the apostle Paul urges, "Give yourselves completely to God—every part of you . . . you want to be tools in the hands of God, to be used for His good purposes" (TLB). Our lives are to be fully given to Him, to be spent any way that He wants. Sometimes pride or independence sneaks in. One time as I was praying for people and prophesying and seeing healings, I felt as though I heard the Lord ask me, "If you kept praying for people and you never saw any more healing, would you be willing to keep praying in this way just because it pleases Me?"

I remember being taken aback, thinking, *Whoa, that's a tough question!* He was asking me, "Even if people weren't being healed, would you keep going for it? Would you still keep pursuing these things?"

It dawned on me in that moment that all the results were for Him, not for me, and they showed His mercy toward those I was praying for. When I realized this, I was able to pray, "Lord, if it pleases You, I'll continue to do it." I was able to decide in my heart that I would continue to do it for Him, no matter what. At the next meeting I attended, I prayed and not one of the first five people I prayed for got healed. My first thought was, *Oh no, it's started! Not only did the Lord ask me that question, but He's actually going to do it!* About four hundred people were at that meeting, and it was a little embarrassing. I had already resolved in my heart, though, that I would model obedience no matter what the results, so I just kept going for it, wondering if this was how it would be from now on.

Have you noticed in Scripture that Jesus never gives His disciples any clue what will happen next? He starts with a simple invitation: "Follow Me." They might have wondered, "Follow Me" to do what? "Follow Me" for how long? But Jesus doesn't say. They just knew that where He was, they wanted to be.

Following Jesus doesn't necessarily mean waiting in your room, fasting night and day, and asking God for special instructions on what you're supposed to do next. I believe that as we walk through life and go about our day, we're called to respond to situations with God's grace, love and the authority that Christ gave us. Simply knowing that God is with us and acting on that knowledge is enough to bring a huge amount of transformation that would be impossible any other way.

Faith is always mixed with perseverance, and it pays to persevere. I don't think God was holding back on me in that meeting, but it did serve as a great test for my heart. At that point, a breakthrough happened inside me that brought me to the place of realizing, *Okay, if the supernatural isn't there, I'm still fine. But I know it's supposed to be there, and I know it's God's will to heal. As long as God is honored, and as long as I know that it's His will and that I'm doing what He wants done, so be it.*

It's not about accomplishing what we want to see or about our version of success; it's about saying, "I'm willing to be used by God in this moment, and the results are up to Him, not me." One way to think about it is that we are meant to be nickels in God's pocket, like loose change He can spend any which way He chooses. He can spend us on big things or small things.

That doesn't mean we sit around and do nothing, of course. We need to choose intentionally to go do what Jesus did. We need to intentionally engage in the Kingdom as His heirs. I held a meeting for a pastor friend of mine, and afterward he said he was concerned about the way that I'd encouraged the young people to go *look* for people to pray for. "If you don't get a direct word from God to pray for a person's healing, then you better not do it," he said. "I don't want my youth praying for people willy-nilly!"

"Send the youth to me, then," I said, "because I do!"

All through the New Testament, Jesus told us to go heal the sick without any qualifications. I think waiting on direct orders with the kind of thinking that says, *I have to have a word or a directive to go*, is slavery mentality. Jesus made us joint heirs with Him. Break the chains of slavery thinking and just go do the things He did!

Practical Steps to Risky Evangelism

Although evangelism can seem risky at times, I want to share with you some easy, practical steps that can help you do what Jesus did with more boldness. Remember what I said earlier? You can be confident that God is present in a situation simply because you are there and He is in you. And the power of the Kingdom can break in to any situation. When you are willing and available, God can do it through you. Here are some steps to take to get started living a risky but effective evangelistic lifestyle.

The Prayer Approach

There really is no limit to the kind of approaches you can use to evangelize. We'll look at several, but to start with, an offer of prayer is a great approach. Wherever you are and whomever you meet, almost everyone around you has things going on that they need prayer for. Prayer is general enough that most people are willing to receive it, and it also gives you an opportunity to invite God into a conversation and let Him take the lead. When you step out and ask people if you can pray for them, at the least they tend to feel loved and cared for.

For me, the best approach has been to simply walk up to anyone and everyone and say, "We're just walking around town looking for people to pray for. What can we pray for you about? Do you have any pain or sickness? What about family or relational needs? Do you need a job or finances? We'll pray for anything."

Most people won't feel comfortable sharing right away and will say something like, "No, I'm good." I expect them to say no at first, and my follow-up question is to simply ask, "Well, could I just pray a prayer of blessing for you right now?" Very few people say no to that even if they aren't willing to name a specific request. I find that offering prayer is the most direct approach to evangelism, without too much beating around the bush or having people wonder what you're getting at.

At the Mall or Shopping

I took some kids from the youth group to the mall one day, and we saw that the Asian nail salon was packed. I told the younger teenage girls we had along to approach the owner of the salon, who was clearly Buddhist, and ask if they could offer her patrons "free peace-soaking prayer." The owner loved it and invited the girls in. She announced to her patrons that the girls would be making their rounds and that anyone who wanted prayer should let the girls know. Out of about ten men and women receiving salon treatments, only one said no. The girls gave many prophetic words and prayed for healing over the people in the shop. The owner invited them back anytime to offer more "free peace-soaking prayer."

Another couple of women from our church go on evangelism shopping trips at Target or the mall. They say to people, "Hey, we're practicing giving encouraging words from God at our church. Could we practice with you?" This is really effective because where some people might feel defensive about receiving from you, they're often glad to "help you out" by letting you practice on them. These two ladies then ask God to give them specific encouragements for the people who say yes, and they ask Him for insights about who the people are and what situations they're facing. The shoppers have been blown away by some of the "encouragements" that have come through these evangelistic women.

Public Transportation

Trains, planes and buses are great places to evangelize because you have a captive audience of people who really don't have much to do while they're riding to their destination. Here's an approach to take while using public transportation: Ask the Lord to show you something specific for a person around you. A girl named Nicole from our church was sitting on a train in Chicago, and she began to pray, "Lord, if You wanted to use me to speak to that girl across from me, what would You say?"

Nicole closed her eyes, and a few different pictures came to mind. Even though they seemed sort of random and disconnected, she took a risk and said to the girl, "You might think I'm the 'crazy lady on the bus' or something, but I think God has given me some pictures for you, and I want to share with you what I'm hearing."

The girl on the bus nodded slowly. Nicole was so nervous about the girl's reaction that she looked down the whole time she was sharing. When she looked back up again, the girl had tears streaming down her face and was leaning forward, listening intently. The images God gave Nicole ended up being very significant words for this girl.

Interviewing and Hobbies

One guy from our church, Jay, was really interested in film, and he used his hobby for evangelism. He went to downtown Naperville with a few friends and started asking people if he could interview them for his documentary. He would ask questions about whether they'd ever experienced God and whether they believed in prayer. It was amazing how many people who didn't go to church and didn't consider themselves Christians still came up with one or two dramatic stories about a time when they had prayed or asked God for something, and they saw Him show up in their lives.

The interviews Jay did around his film hobby stirred numerous spiritual conversations with people about faith. Afterward, Jay and his team would ask the people, "Can we pray right now, ask God to show up and see what happens?" So many cool interactions took place because of Jay's approach. You can experience the same thing if you creatively use one of your hobbies to engage people.

Servant Evangelism

One time while leading a Power Evangelism Conference in Fort Collins, Colorado, we were doing a combination of servant evangelism and power evangelism in the downtown area. Many of the teens with us were scared to ask people if they could pray for them, but they weren't afraid to ask if they could clean their toilets. My friend Steve Sjogren calls this kind of approach "evangelism for chickens." I approached the manager of the largest New Age shop in town and asked if we could bless her and pray that she prosper.

We began to do what I call "repackaging," which means to take what someone gives you to pray for and restate it in a healthy way. We started to pray, "Lord, bless this shop manager. Let the best that You have for her and for the employees be known here. We pray that Your love and presence overwhelm this place." While I was doing this, the kids were scrubbing the shop's toilets. I then prayed, "Lord, come even now and overwhelm this manager with a sense of Your presence and love as never before."

As I was praying and the kids were scrubbing, the manager began to shake all over. She asked, "What's happening to me?"

I told her, "The Father loves you, and you're feeling His presence come over you."

She said, "But it feels like a tug-of-war is happening inside my body!"

I told her, "God wants to love you, but something that's not of God is trying to stop it." I then asked, "Do you want God's love to win?"

"Yes, please!" she answered.

I began to bind and break the demonic power that was trying to hold her back from the love and peace God had for her. She instantly stopped shaking, but started to sweat—a sign of deliverance. She smiled and stated that now she felt a strong peace. I explained that she could continue to enjoy that peace if she would accept Christ. She was willing, and she prayed with me.

I went back to Fort Collins several months later and popped into the shop again, where they told me that the manager had quit the store. She had gotten to the point where she no longer felt comfortable working there.

If talking and praying with people makes you nervous, maybe service evangelism is a good approach for you. Offering to serve people in some way often leads to a spiritual conversation, which can then lead to seeing the Kingdom break in to someone's life.

Treasure Hunt

Some people use what's called the "treasure hunt" model. Kevin Dedmon, a former Vineyard pastor who now serves at Bethel Church in Redding, California, wrote a great book on this topic, *The Ultimate Treasure Hunt*.[2] People who feel most comfortable following concrete, step-by-step directions find that this approach is a great tool.

Before you go out in a group of two or three, pray together and ask God for specific descriptions of people, names, locations and other clues. We did this in Puerto Rico, and one of the worship leaders present got pictures of a hospital, a room number 231, a woman and a heart condition. A group drove to the hospital and asked for room 231. The worship leader asked the two women in the room, "Which one of you has a heart condition?" One of the women raised her hand, so they went over and prayed for her. She immediately felt a physical change in her heart. At first her heart began to race, and then it began to calm down and she noticed that its rhythmic pattern had changed.

At the Gym

I used to go to the gym every day, where I'd constantly pray for people who had different injuries. I asked the Lord for encouragements or words of knowledge for the people I saw there. Whether or not you get a dead-on word that leads to a life change in that very moment, people still remember that God had a word for them.

After one lady with only three months to live was healed of terminal cancer, I got the reputation around the gym of being the "man of God" or the "preacher man." Some believers find it irritating to be labeled like that, but I believe part of what we're called to is being known for our association with Him. The reality is that even people who use those names in a slightly ironic or teasing tone will remember what you stand for, and when they have an issue, they'll come to you for prayer.

A couple of guys at the gym finally had me leading prayer for them every morning. This was entirely on their initiative, and they kept inviting more and more people to join us. It got to where every day around 5:30 a.m., a dozen guys would gather and I would read some Scripture and pray. A gym is a great place for people to get to know you, and through you get to know the God you serve.

Quenching the Thirst

Being salt and light is one of our roles as Christ followers. Our society is becoming more and more secularized, yet people everywhere are feeling increasingly thirsty—and it's a spiritual thirst. We have the answer to quenching that thirst, and we are nickels in God's pocket that He can use in any way He chooses to let people know about His thirst-quenching Living Water.

God puts His Spirit in each of us so that we can be His priests and the pastors of our workplace, gym, favorite mall, public transportation route or school. As we step into a lifestyle of risky evangelism, we can use many creative approaches that work in different ways with different people. We're simply available to go and do what Jesus did, and the Holy Spirit is the ultimate evangelist as we permit Him to work through us.

6 // God Speaks

Learning to Recognize His Voice

> For God, who said, "Let there be light in the darkness," has made this light shine in our hearts so we could know the glory of God that is seen in the face of Jesus Christ.
>
> We now have this light shining in our hearts, but we ourselves are like fragile clay jars containing this great treasure. This makes it clear that our great power is from God, not from ourselves.
>
> 2 Corinthians 4:6–7 NLT

I was on a ministry trip in Siberia a few years ago with some other pastors, one of whom was my friend Chris Simmons from England. We were eating dinner at a venue with a restaurant, coffee shop and bar all connected together. Chris nudged me and nodded over to the corner. "You see that man? That's the former communist leader of Siberia."

I was impressed. When Chris asked if I wanted to meet him, I said sure.

Chris walked me over and introduced us. "Robby, this is Victor." We talked back and forth a little, then Chris said, "Robby is, like, a prophet from Chicago. He's about to tell you things about your life nobody knows." Then he turned and looked at me (they were both staring at me), and he said, "Have a go at him, Robby."

Talk about being on the spot. I looked at the man and said, "All right, let me tell you what I see." The truth is, I had absolutely nothing to say. I started speaking, just trusting God that He'd fill my mouth. Honestly, that's how it works best for me.

I looked at Victor and said, "When you were a little boy, an older woman taught you about Jesus and you believed it. But as you went to school, you began to believe in atheism because that's what they taught. You walked away from believing in Jesus. And I see two times that God saved your life. The Lord personally intervened for you. One involved a fire on a boat where you almost died, and one involved a car accident. Does that make sense to you?"

Victor looked down and shook his head. I saw that and thought, *Oh no, that's a bad sign.*

Then he squinted back up at us and said, "When I was a little boy, my grandmother taught me about Jesus, and I believed it. But in school, they taught me about atheism. Then I believed that. I walked away. Years ago, I was on a Soviet ship that caught fire. The fire began to spread into my cabin. I was able to push several other shipmates in my cabin through the porthole to get them out. My shoulders were too broad, though, and I couldn't get through the opening. All I could do was hang my arm and head out to breathe the little bit of air coming through. Black smoke bellowed out, and I couldn't see through my tears or through the smoke—I couldn't see anything. My eyes were burning; my lungs were burning. All my shipmates were down in the water below me.

"I said, 'Jesus, if You're real, save me now.' As soon as I said that, I felt somebody wrap their hands around my arm and pull me through the porthole. Suddenly I was falling down into the water, even though there was no place for anyone to stand outside that ship. Who pulled me out? When I hit the water, my shipmates asked me the same question. The black smoke was so thick that they couldn't see anything, but they knew there was no place for anybody to stand. I couldn't believe it and couldn't understand how it had happened. Several others died in the fire, but I didn't. There was no way to explain how I was pulled out."

Next Victor told me about the second incident: "Two weeks ago, my wife and I were driving down the highway in Siberia, and a truck began sliding sideways toward us. In Siberia the snowdrifts on the side of the road can be ten feet tall, and they freeze into a solid wall of ice. The truck plowed into the ice and kept coming toward us. Just at the point of impact, I gripped the steering wheel and said, 'Jesus, help us!' All of a sudden, without any idea how it could've happened, we were within an inch of the truck with not a scratch on us or our vehicle. When I close my eyes and think back through every detail of the situation, I still can't explain it."

Victor stopped and looked at me intensely. "You're saying Jesus did this? He saved us?"

"Yes," I said. "He wants a relationship with you, and He's inviting you to have a relationship with Him right now!"

Then Victor said something interesting: "Well, we're all children of God. We don't have to choose that. We're already it. God created us all, so we're all His children. We don't have to make a choice for Jesus."

And then the Holy Spirit just kicked in. I looked at him and said, "Let me ask you a question." His wife was sitting right there, so I asked him, "Did you and your wife choose each other? Or were you chosen for each other by someone else?"

He looked at me strangely. "No, we're not from somewhere with arranged marriages. We made the choice. I chose her." He looked over at her. "She's very proud that I chose her."

I said, "Yes! In that same way, Jesus wants to be chosen. He wants us to choose Him."

Victor looked down as he thought about it, and suddenly he slammed his hand on the table and said, "Then I choose Jesus!"

I can't explain it, but you could feel something pop in the air. It was as though when his hand hit the table, something broke in the atmosphere. Something broke over the area. Victor began to cry. In the minutes that followed, he prayed and gave his life to Christ. It was one of the most powerful experiences I've seen. When we first walked over, I would never have guessed something like this was going to happen. There was nothing about him or the situation that would suggest he was a man in hot pursuit of God, ready to give his life for Jesus. The reality was that God had been pursuing *him* his whole life.

When we walk with the expectation that God wants to break in, we're walking in agreement with the spiritual reality that Jesus declared when He said the fields are white for the harvest (see John 4:35 NKJV). His promise to us is that we will reap where we did not sow. God is the one in pursuit of His people, and we simply walk in the expectation that He is present with us and is at work. In that moment, in that time, expecting that God will show up, we have no idea what the results will be. We expect God to show up because He wants to. He is in pursuit of people through us.

Not Like Dumb Idols

We follow a God who speaks. The record of Scripture shows a God who knows how to communicate. Christianity is a relationship. Cover to cover, the Bible is about God talking to His people. God is not like mute idols that don't speak (see 1 Corinthians 12:2).

When I was younger, the idea of God "speaking" conjured up images of a voice from heaven shaking the room, or maybe words being unmistakably breathed in my ear. I remember the first time it dawned on me that God was able to communicate with us personally, through unique means. I was about twenty years old. One day, a woman in our Christian community approached me lovingly. Her name was Theresa Scott. She commented, "Robby, I feel the Lord showed me that you really need to be careful with your girlfriend. It's becoming something that it's not supposed to be, where your sense of value is coming from your relationship with her. God has far better for you."

It may sound simple, but I remember at the time really knowing it was from God and knowing that He knew what was going on in my mind and heart. I respected this extremely kind and gracious woman so much. I remember looking at her, amazed, and asking, "How did you get that?"

She said, "I was having my devotional time and praying in tongues. I got quiet listening to the Lord, then He spoke to me and I saw that." She told me, "You know, if you pray and ask God to help you get quiet, the Lord will show you stuff. . . ."

I was blown away, thinking, *Wow, I had no idea! I thought that only came through Scripture and prayer.* I couldn't believe hearing from God that way was a possibility for anybody, and nobody had ever told me how to do it. I mentioned it to my mom, and she was really casual about it. She had been doing it for years. It got my wheels turning, and I thought about it for a few years and kind of processed it.

My conviction today is that God is always speaking and communicating with us in different ways. It's a constant thing. We grow in intimacy with Him and learn to recognize the way He speaks to us. In addition, training ourselves to hear His voice for other people is a powerful way to help them connect with His love for them. The classic Christian writer Brother Lawrence was known for his humility and intimacy with God. He wrote to one of his friends,

> It is possible for us to live in the very sense of the Lord's presence, under even the most difficult circumstances. If you and I are going to enjoy the peace of paradise during this life we must become accustomed to a familiar, humble, and very affectionate conversation with the Lord Jesus.[1]

God Speaks through Scripture

The primary and eternal way God speaks is through Scripture, called *logos*. Jesus held Scripture in the highest regard, affirming its divine inspiration, infallibility, final authority and sufficiency.[2] *Rhema* is a specific word for a specific situation. *The New International Dictionary of New Testament Theology* puts it this way: "Whereas *logos* can often designate the Christian proclamation as a whole in the NT [New Testament], *rhema* usually relates to individual words and utterances."[3] The *Expository Dictionary of New Testament Words* by W. E. Vine states,

> The significance of *rhema* (as distinct from *logos*) is exemplified in the injunction to take "the sword of the Spirit, which is the word of God," Eph. 6:17; here the reference is not to the whole Bible as such, but to the individual Scripture which the Spirit

brings to our remembrance for use in time of need, a prerequisite being the regular storing of the mind with Scripture.[4]

Through constantly reading the Word of God, we learn to recognize His voice. Most often He speaks to us directly through this unchanging source. Many times while you're reading the Bible, certain passages will pop off the page as if highlighted. Rather than treating this casually, keep a record as this happens, which is a great way to begin recognizing the way God speaks to you. When you sense that a particular passage is something the Lord may be saying to you, write it down. Spend time praying over that Scripture. Write down what you feel the application from the Lord is, and ask God if there's anything else He wants to speak. Even if you're not sure you're hearing from the Lord, write down the first impressions that come to mind. Trust that He wants to speak. If it's from the Lord, it will bear fruit in your life.

A second confirmation comes from other believers. As you sense God highlighting certain passages and speaking them into your life, share what you're sensing with other believers who are close to you. God designed us to experience Him in community; He'll often confirm what He's speaking to you through other believers, especially people with whom you have accountability relationships.

There's a safety in Scripture because we already have the guarantee that "All scripture is God-breathed and is useful" for building us up (2 Timothy 3:16; see also Isaiah 55:11). As you keep a record of these things over time, you can look back and begin to see patterns emerge of where God has spoken and where He has affirmed or fulfilled His words.

A good way of growing in hearing God's voice for other people is to pray for them and then spend time listening. Read

Psalms and ask God to highlight a passage He would speak for someone. Good questions to ask when you read Scripture or pray for a person are, "Lord, how do You want to encourage this person? How do You see this person? What do You like about this person?" We know from Scripture that God wants to speak to us to build others up, encourage them and comfort them (see 1 Corinthians 14:3). Share what you hear with the person and ask for feedback. The person might readily confirm that this is the same thing he or she has been sensing from the Lord.

As you continue to step out in this area, it may help to keep a record of what happens and the ways you are recognizing that God speaks to you. He is pleased when we take time to seek His direction and guidance. He desires that we grow in intimacy with Him, and He says, "My sheep hear my voice" (John 10:27 NKJV).

A Common Misconception

Many Christians don't believe that they can speak prophetically to others. "What if I don't have the gift of prophecy?" they ask, a question that results from a common misconception about prophecy. They're thinking of someone who operates in the office of prophet, as mentioned in Ephesians 4:11, and they're confused about the more general ability to prophesy, which 1 Corinthians 14 talks about. In the New Testament and still today, many people operate in the general gift of prophecy that encourages, builds up, comforts and edifies people.

Some Christian circles seem to skip over the gift of prophecy because of its frightening implications—in the Old Testament, delivering a false prophecy meant you were stoned. In the New Testament, the people listening simply judged whether or not they believed a prophecy was from God.

There's also some concern about the way prophecy has wrongly been used to manipulate or spiritually abuse others. At the opposite extreme, other Christian circles have idolized prophecy, placing it on a pedestal almost "above the law," which is unscriptural. We are taught to test everything and to judge every word.

I believe the healthiest way to view prophecy given in the general sense is to handle it as we do any other gift—it should be joyfully embraced by the Church, pastored, trained, developed and held to the same standard of accountability. A helpful comparison might be made to the gift of hospitality, which most Christian circles don't find intimidating or overwhelming. In the same way that everyone is admonished to practice hospitality, but some are noted as having the particular gift of hospitality, so it is with other gifts like prophecy. In 1 Corinthians 14:1 (ISV), Paul says we should eagerly desire this gift in particular, implying that asking for it is a prayer request God loves to answer: "Keep on pursuing love, and keep on desiring spiritual gifts, especially the ability to prophesy."

In the Old Testament, God spoke through the prophets to reveal new doctrine. "In the past God spoke to our ancestors many times and in many ways through the prophets" (Hebrews 1:1 GNT). In the New Testament, we see three major purposes laid out for prophecy. It's given first to comfort, strengthen and exhort believers, second as a sign for unbelievers and third to give direction (see 1 Corinthians 14:2–5; 24–25; 1 Timothy 1:18; 4:14).

Other Ways the Father Speaks

Remember that I'm not focusing here on the particular office of prophet, but on the ability of all Christians to recognize and respond to the voice of God as a natural part of being in relationship with Him. We should eagerly seek to grow in this gift. My purpose is to empower and encourage every believer in the many different ways the Father speaks. I also want to equip every believer to prophesy with more confidence and clarity, especially for the purpose of bringing light and hope to a hurting world.

Sometimes when we think of God speaking, we think of dramatic instances like open visions or angelic visitations, but God speaks to us in many ways, and we often overlook some of them. I want to tell you about some of the ways I've recognized God speaking. See if any of these have happened to you. If they haven't yet, remember that they could!

"Popping" Words or Scriptures into Our Minds

I took a prayer team from my church to Los Angeles one year. Along with about two hundred people, we were at a conference I was doing for three Iranian congregations. A tiny woman on our team called out a young guy from the crowd. This was her first time ever doing any type of prayer ministry in that kind of setting, and she said to him, "I'm just getting the word *Beatles* in my mind."

Beatles? we wondered. We looked at her; we looked at him. How could that be a prophetic word? But the guy dropped his head, and tears started rolling down his face. It turns out that everybody had been making fun of him at school because he played bass for his church's worship team. They would mock him when he couldn't do things with them because he had worship practice, and they'd say, "Oh yeah, you gotta go practice with the Beatles!" It meant so much to him that God knew what he was going through. It was as though in a single word he heard the message from God, "I see the suffering and sacrifice you endure for Me."

Popping words can be the simple things that come into our heads. When we ask God to speak, we're trusting the first thing that comes to mind. Sometimes it's more significant than we could have imagined.

On the other hand, don't go fishing with a word that's on your mind: "I see the name Fred—do you have a brother named Fred? No? How about a cousin? A friend? Have you ever met *anyone* named Fred?" I'm being facetious, but the idea is that if it's from God, He'll make it clear. You don't have to fish for the meaning. If you get a word and the purpose seems unclear, just move on. It may be that as you're praying, or even a few minutes later, the meaning will become obvious.

"Popping" Pictures into Our Minds

Often God's prompting can come as a quick flash of images, maybe of something we weren't expecting to think about. When I train people, I tell them to pray over their minds, ask God to speak and trust the first thing that comes. Often it can be a quick picture, similar to imagining something or the way you get an idea. It's easy for us to discount these pictures, but keep in mind that God is infinitely creative and specific in the ways He reaches people.

Years ago, three sisters came to our church in Aurora. One of them had stomach cancer. She was a more casual Christian, but she'd heard that at the Vineyard church in Aurora you could be healed of cancer, so she came and brought her sisters with her. One of them wasn't a Christ follower and the other was. The sister who was a Christian was highly skeptical about the Holy Spirit's activity and healings, and she was concerned that her ill sister was making a big mistake by coming. But the sister with cancer had begged them to come along, and they wanted to support her and make sure nothing too weird happened.

As we prayed for the sister with cancer, she felt a sensation of electricity in her stomach, and she ended up completely healed. While God was obviously touching her, we asked her unbelieving sister if we could pray for her, too. She said, "I guess, but I'm not a Christian."

We started praying for her, and she started leaning farther and farther back. Her eyes were open the whole time, and then she started shaking all over. She kept leaning back almost to the point where it looked as if she'd snap in half. She later said it felt like electricity going all over her body.

Watching her, I got concerned and asked, "Does that hurt?"

"No, this feels great!" she said.

"Really? Are you sure?" I asked.

"Oh yeah!" she said. "I feel great!"

Her position looked so awkward that I asked, "Do you want to sit or lie down?"

"No, no, don't push me down," she replied.

"I won't push you down," I said. "I just want to make sure you're comfortable."

"Oh, I'm comfortable, I'm fine," she said. "There's just one problem—I don't believe in this!"

I told her, "That obviously doesn't seem to be a problem in this situation."

At the end of the service, that unbelieving sister wound up giving her life to Christ as a result. The third sister, the Christian one who was completely skeptical about healing, had heard about the Vineyard and all the strange things we did, so she had come to make sure her sisters didn't get too far into something unhealthy. We prayed for her, too, and gave her a number of prophetic words. She acknowledged them as accurate, but nothing was making a difference for her. Her face looked stone-cold.

A woman named Debbie on our prayer team told her, "I'm getting a picture of a mantel, and on the mantel is a jack-in-the-box. You go and take it off the mantel and just play it over and over again."

At that point I looked at Debbie, hoping she had something much more profound and spiritual to go from. She said that picture was all she had, so I started praying frantically for some interpretation or Scripture to help justify us to this woman who already thought we were weirdos.

As I was thinking all of this, I suddenly saw tears start rolling down the woman's face. Shocked, I asked her, "Does that actually make sense to you?"

She shared, "When I was a little girl, my parents used to fight terribly. They'd throw things—even throw knives at each other. They'd try to hurt each other, and they'd beat each other. It'd get so bad that the only way I could feel any peace was by going next door to my neighbor's house. On the mantel was a jack-in-the-box. I would sit down with it in my lap and play it over and over again just to feel safe." She looked down. "I think God is telling me this is a safe place, too. It's safe here."

Nothing I could have said, no Scripture I could have quoted right then, would have had the same impact on her as that picture. It was an incredible word, and I've told this story for years. Sometimes the picture God gives doesn't make sense to us. There's a fine balance between asking for clarity or interpretation and resisting the temptation to try to make sense of it ourselves. We approach God with faith that He will speak. When we get a word or picture, we can pray for an interpretation or ask if there's anything else He wants to say, but sometimes what we got is all we get. We must only speak what we think God is showing us—it's not up to us to make sense of it or drive it home. We don't have to try to spiritualize it or create an elaborate prayer around it. That actually can dilute the message for the individual because it was God's direct communication to them just the way it came. We need to just say what we see.

Dreams

When people tell me, "I've got a loved one who doesn't know the Lord," one of the things I pray is, "God, invade the person's dreams. Reveal Yourself, speak to them and bring clarity. Give them angelic visitations in the night." God has spoken to me through dreams and angelic visitations numerous times.

I've told so many spouses whose partners are not Christian to pray over their partners' pillows. I've heard story after story of how God has worked through that and brought dreams to the spouses that they couldn't ignore.

The Spirit Bearing Witness

The Spirit will often bear witness that what someone is saying is from God. This is similar to insights or tugs at our hearts. It can occur as we're sitting in silence, or it can occur through things happening around us. In Jeremiah 18, the prophet talks about watching a potter shape a wheel. Suddenly the word of the Lord comes, and God speaks directly to him about the future of Israel.

This witness the Spirit brings can come even through watching a movie, reading a book or listening to a conversation. Often it feels as if everything becomes highlighted or jumps out at you. It may occur in physical circumstances—in nature or even in the middle of traffic. God is always speaking. Sometimes you hear something and you know, *Oh, that's from God.* What Jesus told the woman at the well was a simple revelation. It wasn't new information for her. Anyone who knew her could have told her the same thing. It wasn't the information that was necessarily significant, but because it was a word from God, it penetrated her heart and bore fruit in her life. She recognized Jesus as a prophet, and she felt intimately known and seen by God. She later told everyone, "He told me everything I ever did" (John 4:39).

I believe in that moment, Jesus modeled for us what collaboration with the Holy Spirit truly looks like. A fortune-teller may be able to tell you your driver's license number or what you had for dinner, but it won't change your life. The enemy comes to steal, rob and destroy, but the Spirit comes to give life. A word from the Lord may be as simple as, "God loves you." When it's from the Spirit, it will bear fruit. As we reach out, He confirms and the Spirit bears witness.

Physical Sensations or "Sympathy Pains"

Randy Clark and his ministry have made a huge impact on me. Randy always says, "Pay attention to your body." Many times when we're praying for people, we'll get what we call "sympathy pains." They can be described as temporary, prophetic manifestations of pain or discomfort someone else is experiencing from a condition he or she has that needs healing.

Every time I receive a sympathy pain, I believe God reveals it to heal the condition. I stop and ask the person if I can pray for whatever it is. Sometimes when I'm in front of a large audience, I get specific pains that I describe to everyone; then I call people forward who are experiencing a similar issue.

Tips for Praying for People

When you pray for people you don't know, it's good to remember that the concept of being prayed for can take some people by surprise or even totally disorient them. Most times I say something reassuring like, "God's here, and He wants to bless you. I'm going to pray, and you'll feel His presence come on you so that you can experience Him. He'll also give me words or encouragement for you."

Even if people don't believe in God, it can help them to know what it is you think you're doing. Gauge where people are at, and help them be as comfortable as possible with the situation so they can relax and feel more natural. If things suddenly feel awkward, acknowledge it by saying, "This feels a little awkward, doesn't it?" Ask questions about what they're experiencing. Be kind and be accessible. It's okay to be yourself and be sensitive, but speak boldly.

Call Out the Best God Has for Someone

It doesn't matter how hurting or broken a person seems. God put His image into every single person on earth, so every person you meet uniquely expresses something about Him. There's hidden treasure there.

If I'm talking to prostitutes or a drunk on the streets, I ask the Father, "What's Your heart for this person?" I often tell people going out to minister, "Dig for the gold, not the dirt." Don't try to give words revealing sin or failures.

The dirt might impress people with my gift of the prophetic, but it doesn't impact an individual's life for the best—it just makes them feel exposed. Nobody who has a gold mine says, "Look at all the dirt I've found!" What I pull out of my pocket is all the gold nuggets I've found. Always protect people's dignity.

Put the Responsibility on You, Not on God

No matter how clearly I hear God speaking or how strongly I sense that what I'm getting is from Him, I always package it in a way that puts the responsibility on me. I use phrases like, "I think God is saying . . . I feel God is showing me . . . I sense God is telling you . . . I see . . . I hear . . ."

We want to keep things subjective because it creates a safer environment for people. Every prophetic word is subject to judgment. Whether a person receiving a word is a believer or not, it's up to that person to weigh whether or not it's from God.

Some Christian circles have employed more of an Old Testament prophetic style that comes across as, "Thus sayeth the Lord. . . ." If something is really from God, the power will be in what He's actually saying and in His Spirit confirming it, not in the way we phrase it.

Clarity Is Sometimes a Process

We want moving in the prophetic to be an open process accessible to feedback, while at the same time remaining aware that sometimes it takes a little while for a word to develop clearly. When you feel as though you have a lead with something God may be speaking, be willing to go with it a little even if it initially appears wrong or unclear. It's a balance. Be willing to admit that you could be totally wrong, yet at the same time stay confident that God is speaking and that what you're sensing could be from Him.

I was praying for a woman from France, and I asked her if she had a sister. She said yes, so I shared that I sensed her sister was really struggling with depression and even suicidal thoughts.

The woman said, "No, that doesn't describe my sister at all."

With her permission, I said, "Let me tell you more of what I'm seeing. See if it makes any sense." As I described more of the symptoms and what the whole process behind it had been, she suddenly realized that I was describing exactly what had been occurring with her brother. His abusive circumstances had made me think it was something that had happened to a woman. Once his sister identified what the word from God involved, it resulted in a lot of emotional healing taking place for the whole family.

Relax!

My encouragement is to resist getting flustered. If something doesn't make sense to someone, lean into the word and listen. Relax, trust that God is there and that He is speaking, and try to get a fuller picture. If nothing is coming, stay calm and carry on. It may be that as you continue praying, suddenly you'll get a flash of understanding that brings clarity to the original picture. Or God may bring clarity through a different picture or even through someone else on your team.

Also, realize that we're not perfect. There's not a problem with that. God likes to use us anyway. Enjoy the adventure. We're just called to love people. Whether sharing a spot-on prophetic word or simply asking someone about his or her day, we're called to remain in God's love and let His love remain in us. Keep the main thing the main thing.

Show People Grace

It may be that as you're praying for someone, the Lord will show you an issue He wants to deal with to bring freedom in that person's life. He's looking for people who can handle such words with compassion and love. When dealing with the woman caught in adultery, Jesus' actions drew the attention *away* from exposing or shaming her.

When God gives me pictures relating to any kind of addictive behavior such as alcoholism, pornography, adultery and the like, it's never the thing I start with. After listening to God's voice for encouragement or the true identity He's calling the person to, I might say something like, "I see you fighting this battle. Jesus wants to help you and encourage you in fighting in this battle." Most of the time, I don't even have to explicitly mention the issue. I never even say the word *sin* unless I'm leading the person in a salvation prayer. If the Holy Spirit is bringing the issue up to me, it's because He has already been convicting the person about it. The Holy Spirit has already sensitized the person to it, and the person may already be battling condemnation and accusation from the enemy about it.

The only people Jesus ever talked to about hell were the religious leaders. He came as the advocate for those who feel disqualified and ashamed, and He brings power for breakthrough. We interpret Him saying "Go and sin no more" to sort of mean "Don't you ever do that again!" I believe what He meant was much closer to emancipation. I think it sounded more like, "You are no longer under the power of that sin—you're free to walk away from here and not be bound by the sin that imprisoned you." The Good News of the Kingdom is that we are released from the captivity of sin and its power over us.

Powerful Love

It's important to realize that no matter what you're saying or doing, whether you're getting crystal-clear prophetic words or seeing legs grow out and blind eyes open, the most powerful thing you're doing is ministering God's love to people. I've given very accurate words to people, and they've been totally unmoved. The story I shared of praying for the prostitutes in Puerto Rico exemplifies that. The accuracy of the words I was getting didn't seem to move them, yet when I had them look me in the eye and I said, "Jesus really loves you," that was when they broke down. Everyone who was with me from the church started crying then, too. We all felt the power of God's love breaking in.

God is love, and we want whatever we're doing to demonstrate and glorify His love. The world is dying to hear the message that Jesus loves them, and they don't even realize how much they long for it until you say it.

God Reveals to Heal

Most often when revelation comes about a problem, issue or sickness, it's for the purpose of blessing or healing. Don't simply state the problem or issue; always ask God, "What's Your desire, Lord? What do You want to do in this situation?" If you see a lot of family problems, it's usually because God is about to bring reconciliation, restoration or comfort.

Listen for what God is calling a person to, not just where the person is at in the moment. Words are powerful, and your role may be to declare the blessing that God wants to bring as a way of releasing it to happen. James 4:7 tells us, "Resist the devil, and he will flee from you." In praying for difficult areas, we often stand with people as their advocate, resisting what the enemy is trying to do and declaring God's goodness and love over them.

Revelation, Interpretation, Application

When we get a word or picture, we always ask, "God, what does this mean? What are You speaking through this?" In everything we do, we're asking for the revelation and interpretation, and sometimes we even get the application. Or we may get one of those three, and the recipient may get the other parts. The three parts go together, but sometimes figuring out how they fit can be a process. For instance, once while I was a youth pastor, I had a dream in which I saw a huge bear with a very thick coat of fur in the snow. I shared with the church that I believed it would be a very cold winter and that we should prepare. It ended up being a warmer than usual winter, but on Wall Street it ended up being a "bear market." The revelation was correct, but the interpretation and application were off.

Sometimes we may even get a very strong sense about an application. We don't want prayer to turn into giving advice or counseling, because we're primarily listening to God on behalf of people. But sometimes if we get a sense of an application, we can suggest it to someone.

More Grace than You Realize

Rest in the simplicity of prayer. You may find yourself overwhelmed, wondering, *Okay, is this revelation or interpretation?* Remember it's prayer, so keep it simple. If nothing else, you're simply loving people by praying for them and loving God by obeying Him. That's the powerful part, and it never changes.

The truth is, you'll often find a lot more grace praying for people out in the world than in the Church. Out in the streets, you might blow it trying to hear God's voice or you might not see instant results praying for healing, but people are usually just glad that you tried.

We tend to bicker and judge each other a lot more inside the Church. If you pray for people's healing in church and it doesn't happen, they can get discouraged or mad at God. But I've never had someone who wasn't a Christian say, "That's it, now I know for sure there isn't a God!" People in the world are touched that you stop to listen, give them some attention and try to bring encouraging words. They're usually encouraged that you even cared, so you've already been a demonstration of God's love to them.

Testing What You Hear

Prophetic ministry can be compared to eating fish—savor the meat, but spit out the bones. First Thessalonians 5:19–22 (NIV1984) tells us, "Do not put out the Spirit's fire; do not treat prophecies with contempt. Test everything. Hold on to the good. Avoid every kind of evil." If something is from God, His Spirit will confirm and fulfill it. In a ministry setting like a church where regular prophetic words are being given, some parameters can be set to help maintain healthy boundaries. On the streets, we want to make sure that we empower people to affirm what's being said or to reject it. We never want people feeling manipulated or pressured in any way.

People who've never experienced anything like being given a word from God may not know how to respond right away. I've often experienced times when people aren't sure if a word makes sense for them, but a boyfriend or friend next to them will be smiling and saying, "That's exactly what's been going on!" I still submit everything to the person I'm praying for, but if the initial word is not clear to them, it sometimes helps to continue on and elaborate the picture. As more of it fills in, it might suddenly make sense.

We want to make the experience of being prayed for and receiving from God as accessible to people as possible. If we think they might suddenly be feeling weird, it's okay to stop and ask, "Is this making you feel uncomfortable?" Don't make assumptions, but ask questions and let people be a part of the process and go at their own pace. It's a way of showing love, and it helps alleviate some of the fears people have.

The fruits of prophecy are self-validating. A word will not return void if it's from God, but it needs to be handled carefully. It should always be consistent with Scripture and with God's message of love to us through Jesus Christ.

This doesn't mean that words that sound "scriptural" are automatically correct, though. Even Satan quoted Scripture at Jesus, but in the opposite spirit. Ask yourself, *Does this word line up with God's good character? With His love? Is it calling me/ this person closer to Jesus?* God is never belittling, demeaning, harsh or pushy. Satan is also throwing fiery darts of condemnation, jealousy, comparison and pride in our direction. Continue to ask God for discernment.

The Spirit of God will always agree with the unchanging truth of His unchanging Word. That doesn't mean every word can be found in Scripture; God may speak very specifically about situations in someone's life. But a word will always go with the grain of Scripture. Learning to recognize the voice of God through Scripture sharpens our sensitivity to His voice throughout the day. Daily tuning our hearts through the study of Scripture is our best protection against deception and the counterfeit messages of Satan. We don't have to operate in fear of deception— God is a good God who speaks to His children. All throughout Scripture, He loves it when His people ask for direction and guidance, particularly when they're responsively obeying what He has already spoken. If we ask Him to speak, we don't have to fear that He'll allow us to get a deceptive message instead.

Sometimes a good word from God is like a seed in the parable of the sower (see Matthew 13:1–23). Immediately the enemy may come like a bird to steal it away. Or at times, past hurts in someone's heart can grow up to choke it out like thorns. If you find yourself feeling frightened or discouraged, ask for clarification and perhaps prayer from another believer to help you discern what you need to know about a word. Every word of God bears good fruit in our lives (see Luke 6:43–45; 1 Peter 4:11).

Some words require further confirmation and clarity. If you are unsure about a word, it's okay to set it aside and trust that God will confirm it if it's from Him. Once you can acknowledge that the word is from the Holy Spirit, you can receive it in faith. Scriptures say that Mary was blessed because she believed the promises of God for her life and trusted His goodness at work in them. We want to be receptive and faithful stewards of what God speaks to us, but we don't have to be afraid. Words from God never push us or dominate us, but rather, they lovingly invite us toward Him.

7 // Destroying Satan's Works

I found by daily experience, the more I did, the more I might do for God.

—George Whitefield

The reason the Son of God appeared was to declare God's favor and to destroy the works of the devil (see 1 John 3). Two areas of Jesus' ministry I want to touch on briefly are healing in this chapter and freedom from oppressive spirits in the next. I began this book by sharing the story of a man who was dramatically healed by God before open-heart surgery and who received a new lung in the process. At that time, I didn't have faith for healing. In theory, I believed God was able to heal, but I didn't believe He was about to heal in that moment, and certainly not by using me. When I received a report of what had happened after I prayed for that man, no one was more surprised than me. That was two decades ago. Since then, I've seen limbs grow out, people rise out of wheelchairs, cancer leave people's bodies in a matter of hours, tumors disappear and blind men see for the first time. I've seen God use children to heal brand-new believers, skeptics, sick people and even people who aren't sure they believe in God.

God wants to heal. I know many of us have struggled with the question, "I prayed for someone, but they weren't healed. Does that mean I shouldn't pray for healing?" It's a question I can relate to, having prayed for thousands and thousands of people, and having seen many thousands walk away unhealed. I will address this more extensively later in this chapter and in chapter 11, "Doubt Is No Disqualifier," but let me mention here that we don't have control over the results. As I said earlier, the results aren't for us. Many times I've prayed for someone because I know God wants to heal, but since nothing immediate happened, I've had to walk away with no idea of the result. Time after time, however, I've heard reports back of amazing healings or changes that have taken place hours or days after we prayed.

Jesus taught His disciples to pray, "Your kingdom come, your will be done, on earth as it is in heaven" (Matthew 6:10). There's no sickness in heaven, no brokenness, no shame. Wherever Jesus went proclaiming the Kingdom of heaven, people were healed. When we pray for the sick to be healed, we're agreeing with heaven. Jesus was the perfect model of what a life dependent on the Father looks like, yet we never see Jesus questioning God about His will to heal someone. Jesus questioned the Father once, while hanging on the cross. In that moment, He asked why the Father had forsaken Him. But notice Jesus only questioned the Father after He had fully taken on sin and had become as we are. When it came to healing, however, Jesus clearly seemed to know it was the Father's will, and He released it to everyone who asked for it. He showed us what it looks like to walk in authority as a human, doing the will of the Father. He trained

His disciples to walk in this authority, too, and He has given this same authority to us (see Matthew 28:18).

Healing is available to the Church as part of God's blessing to those who put their faith in Jesus. You don't have to be an expert at it—it's not for the spiritual elite. Paul tells us God has "blessed us with every spiritual blessing in the heavenly realms because we are united with Christ" (Ephesians 1:3 NLT). That doesn't mean healing happens all the time. It involves spiritual warfare. Yet even in Nazareth, where only a few of the sick were healed, the implication was still that this is not what God would have wished (see Mark 6:4–5).

Jesus taught us to pray that the Kingdom would come here on earth, so that means there's still a gap between the breaking in of the Kingdom and the fullness of the Kingdom that is to come. Our desire to see the fullness of God's Kingdom and His will being done on earth lines up with God's desire. Healing is one of the basics of the Kingdom message; it's just part of our lifestyle as believers. Not all of us have the particular gift of healing mentioned in 1 Corinthians 12:30 or have a full-time healing ministry. If you want the gift of healing, ask for it—but whether you have it or not, don't let that stop you. We all carry the power and presence of God to heal the sick; it's part of our DNA in Christ, and it's available to each of us. I encourage every believer to step out in this area. Keep at it until you see your first person healed.

Don't get discouraged if you pray for someone and healing doesn't happen, or if you must pray several times. God is not discouraged with you! Just ask yourself, *Do I want to see God heal the sick?* No one wins a war by firing a single bullet; it usually takes many shots. Persevere in praying for sick people, and I guarantee you'll see healing happen. If you want to see it happen even faster, pray for people outside the Church. Our simple acts of faith praying for healing in the environment of the world are like a weapon of mass destruction against the kingdom of darkness. Sometimes it feels more like we're engaged in trench warfare, though. As we've continued to send teams of people to certain areas in our city, we've seen the number of healings grow exponentially. We've come to see certain zones as healing "hotspots" that were originally some of the darkest, most intimidating places to approach. Once the enemy suffers "casualties" in a certain area, it's as if he begins to run screaming the moment he sees us coming.

Healing is God's Kingdom breaking in, and it doesn't come without resistance. James 4:7 says, "Resist the devil, and he will flee from you." Too many times, we miss out on healing and blame a lack of faith on our part or on the part of the person being prayed for. However, I've seen people healed when I had no faith, and I've seen people healed who themselves had no faith. I've also seen people healed when *neither* of us had faith. Whatever the case, just go for it!

"I'm a Healer!"

"Heads up! Heads up! Preacher's a comin'!" the African-American woman hollered to a small group of mostly men lounging by the Dumpsters in the summer sun. The guys perked up, and one of them stood to his feet. I was with a group of young people who were visiting our church from Atlanta. They were doing a week of community service and some training with me on how to pray for people on the streets. Around the corner from our church, on the east side of Aurora, stands a dilapidated three-story boarding house that rents rooms to a lot of down-and-outers. Usually a few groups of people can be found hanging out there during the day, sometimes doing drugs or drinking by the Dumpsters. This woman had been a local for years, often working as a prostitute. She was still a recognizable beauty, though she bore the signs of living a difficult life.

I smiled at her teasingly. "Now, Violet, why do you say that? You act as if you're warning people—like I'm a cop."

She grinned back sweetly with a toothy smile. "I just wanted them all to know the preacher was here. I wasn't warning them."

I nodded to the others hanging around. "Hey, my name's Robby, and I'm here with some friends looking for people who might need prayer for anything." I'd taken groups to pray in this area for years, and it had become sort of a prayer hotspot.

Besides Violet, I hadn't encountered any of these guys before, but this group seemed like a good place to start. The idea of someone having an injury in their left knee popped into my head, so I asked, "Which one of you has a problem with your left knee?" I looked at each of the guys, most of them African American or Hispanic. A young white kid was with them, about nineteen or twenty years old. I asked him, "Is it you?"

He started limping away, saying, "No, no, my knee's fine."

The guy standing beside him hit him on the shoulder. "You're a liar!" he said. "Don't lie to the preacher—God will strike you dead!"

I said, "God's not going to strike you dead, but if your knee's hurting, let me pray for you. God will completely heal you right now."

"What?" He looked up at me confused, not making much eye contact.

"Yeah," I said, "He'll do that because He loves you, cares for you and wants to heal you."

"Well," he started slowly, "I don't got no money anyways."

I told him, "I don't need any money. I don't charge for this." Then I said, "Let me ask you, where are you at right now with pain and tightness on a scale of 1–10, 10 being the worst and 0 being no pain at all?"

He looked down at his leg. "Right now I can't even bend it; it really hurts."

I said, "All right, we'll call where you're at right now a 10." I reached down and touched his knee and said, "Father, thank You for healing power and for my new friend here. In the name of Jesus, knee, I command this knee to be healed right now. I command all pain to get out and this knee to be completely healed so that he knows that You love Him and that You want a personal relationship with him."

Then I stopped and looked at him. Everyone's eyes were glued to his knee. "Bend your knee and tell me where it's at from 1–10," I said.

He bent his knee slowly. He kept bending it and bending it until it went all the way down. He gave me the strangest look, then he put out his foot and put all his weight on the one knee, then did a dip with it. He looked at me and kind of chuckled. Then he did a dip with just the injured knee again and came back up. "Huh," he said, and he took off running down the driveway.

"Come back here!" I called out. "We're not done yet." The guys sitting around were looking after him, half laughing at the whole situation.

He yelled back at me, "You're scary, dude!" and kept running until he turned the corner of the block.

The rest of us, including the kids from Atlanta, just stood there by the row of Dumpsters at the back of the driveway. A fence all along the property separated it from the alleyway, and all of a sudden we heard him running down the alley. He had gone all the way around the block and was running lightning fast toward us. When he got to the fence, he jumped it.

The older African-American guy sitting next to me said, "Now I *know* he's healed!"

I looked at the young man and smiled. He had kind of a wild look in his eyes. I asked, "So, how did that feel? Where are you with the pain on a scale of 1–10? And don't be nice; tell me the truth."

He looked at me, still breathing hard. "Zero."

"You don't have any pain at all? Any tightness?"

He said, "None whatsoever."

The whole situation took me by surprise, because I'd never had anyone run away like that. I looked over at the rest of the guys and asked, "Which one of you has one leg shorter than the other?"

About half a dozen people were around, and the guy who had hit the young man in the arm earlier stepped over to me gleefully. "Look at this," he said, throwing up his arms in front of me. One was a full twelve inches shorter than the other. "You ever seen an arm grow out?"

I had seen backs straighten and fingers grow out, but not like that. The most I'd ever seen grow out was probably an inch. I started praying for his arm, though. We prayed about four times, and nothing changed.

The guy told me he thought it had grown an inch, but I just shook my head and said, "Dude, don't lie. You don't have to help me out."

After we had prayed several times and hadn't seen any results, I asked him again about whether he had a leg that was shorter. That was the original sense I'd gotten.

He said, "Yeah, one of my legs is shorter."

Then I looked at the kid whose knee had just been healed. I said, "Do you want to see God use you to make this man's leg grow out?"

He cocked his head to the side. "I don't know how to do that."

I smiled and said, "I'll help you." We had the guy sit down again and line up his legs to a mark on the ground so we could see the leg that was clearly shorter. Both legs were stretched out against the straight line. I said, "You see that? Take hold of his legs. Now watch that short one move. Repeat after me: 'Father, I thank You for Jesus Christ. I thank You that He died for our sins on the cross. . . .'"

I was sort of squeezing the Gospel message into the prayer, and the kid was repeating it.

"Right now, by the authority Jesus gave us by dying on the cross, leg, I command you to grow out."

The leg started moving. As we all watched, about three-quarters of an inch shot out.

The kid dropped the guy's legs and started shouting, "Oh, my God! I'm a healer and I didn't know it!" The kid was shaking all over.

I just shook my head. "Not exactly, but let's finish. Hold the legs again." We continued praying over them: "Father, I thank You for this leg that just grew out partway, and leg, I command you to grow out the rest of the way right now in Jesus' name!"

The leg grew out until it was perfectly even with the other one. "Now stand up and check it," I told the guy.

He stood up and walked around. "It's normal! It's never been normal!"

Then I told him, "What God just did with your leg, He wants to do for your life. He wants to bring peace, healing and restoration in all the hurt, wounded, uneven parts of your life."

I also looked at the young guy next to me, who was still excited. I said, "You know how God just used you to heal? Now He's offering to use you to help bring that transformation to others for the rest of your life."

I looked around at the whole group. "Do you want to receive that personally and follow Jesus with your lives?" I asked.

Violet responded that she would, and two of the guys and one of their girlfriends said yes as well. Those four gave their lives to Christ that day and ended up coming to an Alpha course we were running at our church, where they explored the basics of living a life of faith and learned how to build relationships in the community.

What If Healing Doesn't Happen?

I mentioned that one of the most common reasons believers don't pray for healing is that they've had the experience of praying for people and not seeing them healed. Yet I've also seen new believers rush out into the street and see God heal half a dozen people through them in an afternoon. Healing can be that simple, instantaneous and apparent. We all wish every healing would happen that way, but many of us grow disheartened and disillusioned when that isn't the case. But no matter how long you've been praying for people to be healed and what kind of results you've seen, a helpful tip is to *focus on what God is doing, not on what He isn't doing.*

As I said, healing involves a spiritual battle, so don't give up. Doubts, fears, uncertainties and mysteries are a normal part of the Christian life. It's part of the tension of the Kingdom, which is "here, but not yet." We can't allow things we don't know or understand to hold us back or rob us of the wonderful things God is doing.

We're especially vulnerable to discouragement when someone close to us is sick and suffering. We can't explain all the circumstances, but we can obey in all circumstances. We know we've been told to heal the sick, even though we don't yet see it happen all the time, every time. That's part of what it means to live not by what we see, but by what we believe. As Alan Hirsch cleverly titled it, it's a "Faith of Leap."[1] Suffering will always be a part of the battle here on earth, but so will victory, so keep praying for people (see John 16:33; Romans 8:17; 2 Corinthians 1:5; 4:8–10; Philippians 1:29; James 5:10). We don't stop praying for those we love if they're not immediately healed. In Luke 18:1, Jesus told His disciples that they should always pray and not give up.

If someone doesn't get healed at a particular time, don't get frustrated. Just move on to the next person, and keep in mind that I've often seen people who are sick or only partially healed become healed themselves as they pray for others. Christ conquered the cross, and with that, He released authority to us. We seek His presence, His Kingdom and His glory. Healing is not a measure of success, nor is it an end in itself—it's simply a part of His goodness and reign. As we continue to seek the Kingdom and proclaim the Good News of God's love and grace, we see more and more breakthrough. Even at the same time as some of the greatest spiritual opposition comes against the Church, some of the greatest power we'll ever experience is advancing God's Kingdom.

No Formula Needed

Power evangelism is not about following a specific formula or method, though hundreds of books have been written on the topic. John Wimber's book *Power Healing*[2] offers a great apologetic that addresses many of the doubts and fears the Church has faced surrounding power healing. It also gives a comprehensive overview of the biblical foundation for healing, as well as providing practical training ideas. My friend Chris Overstreet at Bethel Church has also done a great job writing a simple step-by step manual on how to walk in supernatural evangelism. It's called, appropriately, *A Practical Guide to Evangelism—Supernaturally*.[3] Randy Clark and Bill Johnson have written powerfully on the subject as well. My favorite book on healing is my friend Jack Moraine's *Healing Ministry*.[4]

From famous ministers like Smith Wigglesworth, a powerfully gifted healer with unusual methods, to modern-day Heidi Baker healing the deaf and raising the dead in Mozambique, healing has always been a part of Church history. It has spanned from first-century believers to what's occurring today in the wildfire growth of underground churches in China, Africa and the Middle East, places where Christianity was previously unheard of.[5] The fastest, most dramatic healings I see occur on the streets, often in areas of great spiritual darkness. Vineyard Pastor Jackie Pullinger once asked, "You want to see a revival? Plant your church in the gutter."

Christ said the fields are "white for harvest" (John 4:35 NKJV). This confused the disciples, but Jesus was speaking of a present-day spiritual reality. The problem is not the lack of a power supply in heaven, but the supply of faithful workers willing to go out and speak out in risk. It's not necessarily easy. It often requires perseverance, but God is with us in the process. We've been given the Great Commission, and as we go out bearing the Good News of Jesus Christ, God accompanies us with healings, signs and wonders.

The main thing I've always taught is that if you want to see people healed, you have to keep praying for sick people. Situations where we can pray for people's healing often present themselves to us every day. At work, at school or almost anywhere, people complain about symptoms or illnesses they're experiencing. Make it a habit to stop and pray for them. Just say the words, "May I pray for you right now?" Then follow these steps I'm about to go through—not as a formula, but as an approach that will help you as you step out in supernatural evangelism.

Ask for Permission and Be Clear

Explain to people that you're going to pray right away for God to heal them. Ask permission to place a hand on them, if appropriate. If I'm praying for a woman, I usually ask her husband or her friends to put their hands on her rather than doing it myself. This is sometimes a good idea with children and their parents, too. It's okay if people say no to being touched, but it's worth asking permission since power is often transmitted by touch. Help people feel comfortable by being clear about what you're doing. They're often more open and grateful than you'd expect.

Gather Information

Ask if the people you're praying for are currently experiencing any pain or symptoms. After they describe the issue to me, I ask them to think of the pain on a scale from 1–10, 10 being the level of pain or discomfort they're starting out at before we pray. Sometimes I also ask them to name something they cannot currently do, something they'd see as a sign of healing if they could do it. (Maybe bending a hurt knee or moving in a certain way without pain.) Healing is often a process, so understanding what the issue is and how it's affecting someone helps us know how to pray and be attentive to what God is doing. Listen for any clues about what God wants to do and any sense of how to pray.

Tell the Body What You Want It to Do

I shared a story in chapter 1 about praying for a gangster's short leg with my friend Todd White and how Todd prayed, "Leg, get out here! Bones, muscles, skin, grow right now." Because many believers are used to saying, "I can't heal anyone—only Jesus can," it may sound funny to some to say that we've been given the authority to heal, but it's true. He is in us, and when we pray for healing, we're taking authority and commanding sickness to leave the body. We're taking back dominion in the name of Jesus. We're not asking God, or even begging Him. Think about it—what would happen if a police officer captured a criminal and then called down to the police station to ask the commander to come and arrest the person? The commander would probably yell at the officer for wasting time and say, "You do it! I gave *you* the authority to arrest him."

In the same way, Christ has given us the authority to heal (see Matthew 10:8; Luke 9:1–2; 10:9). We're not battling God for healing; we're battling against the prince of this world and his kingdom of brokenness, sickness and death (see Ephesians 6:12). When I pray for healing, I don't hedge. We can be direct and straightforward, as Todd was when he prayed for that leg, and we can tell the body what to do.

Ask What's Happening/Pray Again

In Mark 8:22–26 we see Jesus praying for a blind man twice. If Jesus gets two times, I figure that gives me at least twelve times, or maybe even thirty chances! There's no need to rush or feel flustered. Just ask the person what's happening, and if needed, pray again. As you pray, people often experience physical sensations of peace, heat, tingling and/or electricity. These can all be different manifestations of the Holy Spirit at work and God making Himself real to them.

When someone's pain is completely gone, I sometimes ask the person to try to do something he or she couldn't do before. Sometimes there's only a partial healing, and the next day the person is fully healed. Other times someone experiences nothing at all, but then finds at the next doctor visit that he or she is completely healed. I try not to worry too much about the results. Even with partial healings, I thank God for what He's doing. My job is to take authority and pray for healing; the results belong to God.

Thank God and Point People to Jesus

This is all about the Father. I always praise God for healing in advance, and I explain that what I'm doing is a demonstration of God's reality, His love for us and His closeness. When people are healed, I often take them with me to pray for their friends, neighbors or other people on the streets so they can see that since they have received, they now have something to give. Doing this illustrates to them how the Kingdom is advanced here on the earth. John Wimber used to say, "We get to give, to get to give, to get to give." We have received, and now for it to grow in us, we need to give it away.

Healing isn't at the center of what we do—God's love is. We take authority over sickness, but what we're ministering to people is the presence of God. There's power in the presence of God for healing and deliverance, but our goal in everything is for people to encounter the reality of God's presence and to experience His love for themselves.

8 // Freedom for the Captives

Darkness cannot drive out darkness: only light can
do that. Hate cannot drive out hate: only love can
do that.

—Martin Luther King Jr.

But if I cast out demons by the finger of God, then
the kingdom of God has come upon you.

—Jesus (Luke 11:20)

When Angie and I moved to Aurora to plant our Vineyard
church, the very first week we arrived everyone in our
home became desperately ill. Within a day of moving into our
new home, we were all nauseous and vomiting. It was horrible.
We had no family in the area. We had no insurance. We had
no medical provision. We didn't know what we were going to
do. We were there to plant this church with only a handful of
people, and none of them were available to help us. Both Angie

and I felt awful, and so did our kids, who were one and three at the time. It took all of our energy to crawl out to our car, load up the kids and head to Walgreens a few miles down the road, hoping to buy something over the counter that could help us somehow. We were in really bad shape.

As we were driving to Walgreens, Angie suddenly slammed her hand on the dashboard and yelled, "Satan, get in this car right now!"

I looked at her, shocked, thinking, *Why on earth would anyone say something like that?* I had never even seen anyone do anything like it.

I watched part in horror and part in awe as my beautiful, blue-eyed wife furrowed her brow and said, "You listen to me, Satan—we're going to plant this church. We're going to plant it with the poor in the worst part of town. We're going to see the Kingdom come. You can fight us all you want, but we won't quit! We will not bow; we will not break. Now, get out of my car!"

I know this sounds hard to believe, but instantly, right in that car, we were all healed. Whether it was the power of a desperate mother defending her family or the power of a daughter of God proclaiming His Kingdom, it worked. The sickness left every one of us. I'm married to a fierce woman of God! That day, Angie taught me something about the authority we have in Christ, something I didn't know we possessed. We carry an immense authority, and most of us aren't even aware of it.

Born into a War

Whether or not you and I acknowledge it, our lives as Christians involve us in spiritual warfare. First John 3:8 says, "The reason the Son of God appeared was to destroy the devil's works." How do we destroy the devil's works? Every time we share the Gospel and lead a lost person to Christ, every time we heal, every time we forgive, every time we bring freedom through deliverance, every time we encourage people or speak truth and freedom and God's love to them, we're destroying the works and lies of the enemy. When we step out in Kingdom work, we're reclaiming what was stolen from humankind after the Fall and extending the Kingdom of heaven.

We all need to recognize that we face spiritual conflict. In my case, I had to go from running away from spiritual warfare to picking fights with the devil. My experiences growing up had left me terrified of the spiritual realm, and in my twenties this was exacerbated by some negative encounters I had in a few Pentecostal circles. I happily felt that I was leaving all that behind when I accepted a job as the youth pastor of a Mennonite church in Illinois. I loved being a youth pastor and working with kids. I could unleash my creativity, and my natural passion for evangelism flourished. The youth group was soon growing quickly, and I felt that things were going well.

After a few months, a girl who was involved in some really strange things began coming to our youth group. She and four of her friends had been hanging around another guy and girl who were really into vampirism. This couple would make little cuts on these girls and drink their blood. The guy had told the girls he was going to put a spell on them. He hypnotised them, and when they were under his control, he told the girls that he was leading them into a room and they were to go inside. When they obeyed, he locked the door. The strange thing was that even afterward, every time these girls closed their eyes they felt as if they were in this room, and dark spirits would come and torment them. When they slept at night, they felt as if they were sleeping in this room, and they would wake up feeling trapped and restless. No matter what they did, they couldn't escape.

One of the girls' dads had been forcing her to come to youth group. Though she didn't want to come at first, she was intrigued by what she saw happening during our meetings. She started telling the other girls about it and added that she thought I might be powerful enough to help them get free from what was happening to them. I remember noticing these girls sitting completely silent along the wall. After the meeting, they asked if they could talk with me. They came to my office and started crying as they told me what was happening to them and how stuck they felt. They said that when they were "locked" in that room, demons would come to them.

This was the first time I'd encountered something of this nature that I didn't try to run from. I felt as though I had to try to help these girls somehow. I said to them, "The Lord can free you from this; it can happen tonight. But if it does, you're going to need to accept Christ or it's going to be worse."

They all said they wanted to accept Christ, so we started praying. They said they could feel the heaviness lifting off. I was feeling something, too—it was the first time I really felt I had authority over demonic power. All of my life, I'd avoided any type of confrontation. It terrified me. Now here I was defending these girls! I was angry at what they had been put through, and I knew that God could stop it.

As we prayed for the girls, one of them started screaming "Nooo! Why did you do that? Why?" She was reacting dramatically to my prayers, and the look in her eyes was one of sheer terror.

I told her, "The Lord can free you from this right now, if you want Him to. We can break this, and it will go."

Still terrified, she yelled, "Don't touch me! Don't touch me!"

As we talked, she started to recognize the connection between the overwhelming feeling she was experiencing and the demonic power, but she wouldn't agree to go further or to tell the spirit to leave. I ended up having someone else from the church take her home to separate her from the other girls. I'd follow up with her later, but I felt that at that moment they needed to be separated.

The other four girls were completely set free and asked Christ to fill them with His Spirit. They got involved in the ministry and matured spiritually. Years later, the girl who brought them ended up coming with us to help with our church in Aurora, and she and her husband served as home group leaders.

Most of us involved in long-term pastoral care have seen Christians struggling with demonic oppression. Paul warns in Ephesians 4:26 against giving the devil a foothold. This applies to all of us. We're told to resist the enemy, and he will flee from us. When we encounter Christians who are battling some form of unclean spirit, regardless of what the issue is or what sin is involved, we don't judge. We minister out of love and mercy, as Jesus did, and as He does for us. Oppressed people don't know how to battle effectively, so we battle for them with no need to fear, because we have full authority in Christ to deal with the issues we face.

Understanding Our Authority

When Jesus sent out the 72 disciples, Scripture tells us that they prayed for the sick and the sick were healed. But what amazed the disciples most of all was the way that demons submitted to them in the name of Jesus. Jesus told them He had given them authority over "all the power of the enemy" (Luke 10:19 NKJV; see also 17–20).

Over all the power of the enemy! Over all demons! I used to tend to be a little more courageous praying for the sick than praying for the demonized. If somebody had a cold, I'd pray for it. But if somebody was screaming and speaking in strange voices, I'd rather call over someone else to take care of it. I was definitely fearful.

We all can feel intimidated, yet Jesus promises that we've been given authority over *all* demons. He didn't promise authority over all sickness, but we have authority over *all* demons. Every time you confront a demonic spirit, walk into the situation with your head up and your shoulders back, knowing the demon has to submit to the name and authority of Jesus and go. Don't step in with fear, and don't be timid. The enemy throws fiery darts of fear at us to hold the Church back, but we're dressed in the authority and righteousness of Christ.

Jesus said the ruler of this world "has nothing in Me" (John 14:30 NKJV). We need to realize that if Christ is in us, then the enemy has nothing in us either. Demons can only go where we give them permission. Where we forbid them from going, they must obey. That's why the subtitle of this book includes "routing" demons. A few years ago, we did a deliverance at our church and forbade any demons from coming through the door again. A few months later, we ran into problems when people reported to us that they couldn't physically enter our church building. They literally felt held back from being able to walk through the church door. We changed our prayer, giving permission for people to enter who had demons but who wanted to be set free. We recognized that our first prayer was too general in forbidding any demons to enter, which prohibited way too many people who sincerely wanted freedom from getting it. I learned through that situation to be more specific when I prayed.

Out on the streets, when you're working with unbelievers who begin to manifest demons in public, you usually take authority over the demon, bind it and shut it down. Typically you're not going to cast it out unless you're in an environment where you can engage the person and know that he or she wants to be set free and come to Christ as a result. Scripture warns that without a person knowing Christ, casting out a demon could lead to even further demonization (see Matthew 12:43–45).

If a demon is flagrantly manifesting and the person seems aware of it, I bind it, command it to go and release peace over the person. When things calm down, I ask the person, "Do you want to be free?" These encounters vary greatly on a case-by-case basis. It may sound strange, but many people are aware of an unclean spirit but are unsure if they want it to go. Some people like the power, thrill or experience a demon gives them. Some have felt empty after being freed from a spirit and miss the feeling. I'll usually tell them something like, "All of this will go right now, *if* you want to accept Christ." Accepting Christ completes the transformation and protects them from any demonic reoccurrences.

Power Struggles Not Allowed!

Never get into a power struggle with a demon—they don't get to do that! The following story dramatically illustrated for me how much authority is actually ours and how the enemy is constantly fighting us, trying to control and intimidate us and keep us from using our authority. About five years after we planted our church in Aurora, a Baptist pastor friend from our area, Dave, called and left several messages on my phone. (I changed his name to protect his privacy.) I had just returned from a trip to Lithuania and was catching up with my phone calls, and his first message sounded somewhat anxious. He said they were dealing with a little situation, and they would like me to come over and pray with them. He left three messages over the course of 48 hours, and by the third message his voice sounded hoarse and exhausted. He told me they were dealing with a woman from their church who definitely had a demon, and he asked me to *please* call him back the second I got the message.

I was a little surprised by Dave's messages because at the time, I knew for a fact that he didn't really buy in to the idea that the spiritual realm was very active in the present day. Still, I could hear this screaming woman in the background, so I called him back and arranged to join him. When we walked in the front door of the apartment where they had the woman, I saw that furniture was strewn everywhere and the place was a wreck. Three men and two women were holding down this little Puerto Rican lady. They'd pinned her to the ground, and she was screaming and writhing. They all looked as if they'd been totally beaten up. At least one of them had a bloody nose. Some of their clothes were torn. An intercessor sitting on the couch was bleeding from the mouth. Mess and clutter were everywhere.

Dave looked up at me and said "Robby! Please help us. I don't care what you have to do, just help us! We can't get rid of this thing."

I then asked him to give me authority to do the deliverance. This is very important. Because he was the woman's pastor, she was in his sphere of influence and under his direct spiritual authority. Deliverance is a power struggle. When doing deliverance, we want to clearly establish lines of authority, with one person in leadership and the others only in supporting roles. Authority comes from God. When we recognize and honor God's delegated authority, we're aligning ourselves with the order of His Kingdom. The enemy, who feeds off chaos and confusion, knows this and must submit to it. Our role is to bring order and peace to a situation.

When I walked into the room, different people were hollering out all kinds of things at the same time, things like "In the name of Jesus . . . ," "The blood of Jesus . . . ," "Fire, burn this demon." Having been at it for days, everyone was exhausted. The demon in the woman was still screaming and seemed to feed off the drama and chaos. The woman herself seemed quite energized.

The pastor had only one request—that we not speak in tongues. I told him, "It may take a bit longer then, but okay."

He told the other guys, "This is Robby. He's a pastor friend of mine. He's going to be in charge. Do whatever he says."

I looked at the guys holding her down and said, "Everybody stop praying and speaking to the demon. Let this lady go."

They looked at me, terrified, and said, "What? She'll beat us up again! Do you see what she's done here?"

I said, "Let her go. I promise you, she won't lay a hand on you." I reassured them again, and they finally let her go. When they did that, the woman, who had been lying on the ground, suddenly rose to her feet without using her arms or bending her knees. It was like someone had stepped on the end of a rake. She did it with her eyes closed.

That kind of sent a shiver down my spine. I said, "Okay, you're not allowed to do that again. I forbid you to do that. Now by the authority of Jesus Christ, you're going to do exactly what I say. This is not optional. You will obey me because this is Christ's authority that He gave me at the cross of Christ. In the name of Jesus, I command you to sit down on that couch right now."

The woman marched right over and sat upright on the couch. The guys' mouths dropped open.

Heaving and fuming on the couch, the woman yelled, "I have more power than that pastor; I have more power than that man. . . ." She kept naming off different people in the room.

I said, "You do not have more power than was given to me on the cross of Christ. Now, stop speaking."

She closed her mouth, but her cheeks kept puffing up as if something was trying to come out but was unable to. The room around us was in complete disarray, and I don't know why it occurred to me at the time, but I said, "You've torn up this woman's home; clean up her house for her right now."

Faster than I've ever seen anybody move in my entire life, she rose and cleaned the entire apartment with her eyes still closed.

I said, "Now, sit down." She did, and again the guys in the room were amazed. I was amazed, too. The pastor asked me, "How did you know you could do that?" I said, "I didn't know but just thought to try it." As we were sitting there, the woman coughed three times, and I noticed that everyone else in the room suddenly coughed in unison the same way. A few minutes later she coughed again, and everyone else in the room immediately coughed the exact same way again.

I asked the pastor, "Did you notice that?"

He said, "Oh yeah, we've all gotten this strange cough the past few days."

I said, "No, watch." I turned to the woman and said, "Do it again." Then she began to cough repetitively—*cough, cough, cough*. Except for Dave and me, everyone mimicked her in unison together—*cough, cough, cough*. The pastor and I looked at each other, wide-eyed.

I wondered out loud, "What's this?"

From within the woman, the demon screamed out, "*I have more power than Fred! And I have more power than Matt!*" The woman named each person in the room.

I looked at the people around the room and asked, "Do you see what she's doing to you with this cough? It's the demon controlling you."

As we moved into prayer and began to take authority over the situation, I asked the Lord, "What's going on here?" (I never get my information from the demon, only from the Holy Spirit.) I sensed in my spirit that the woman had come from a family involved in witchcraft. When I shared this with her pastor, he confirmed, "Oh yeah, she was baptized in a church of Satan. As a child, she was dedicated to the devil."

The woman had accepted Christ, but it was as if part of her was still trapped in a compartment of pain and ritual abuse that needed to be addressed so she could be set free. I started breaking off curses, binding the demon and asking it to leave. Her chest would lunge forward and she'd have a moment of clarity for just a few seconds, then all of a sudden the demon would appear again and growl at us, show its teeth and hiss. Finally it left, and we asked the Holy Spirit to fill her and fill that void.

It took around 45 minutes before the woman was finally sitting on the couch and talking to us normally. We asked if she remembered anything about what had been taking place, and she said she could only recall bits and pieces. Sometimes she was out of her body, watching it; sometimes she was someplace else really dark. We were able to refer her to some friends of ours who are skilled inner healing counselors. They followed up with her, and I still see her around town to this day. She's doing great, and she's one of the sweetest women I know.

I share her story not to freak people out, but to show how much authority is actually ours even when we face some of the most extreme situations. That deliverance session was one of the clearest examples I've ever seen of oppression, control and intimidation getting out of hand. Pastor Dave is now in our church and does powerful deliverance ministry in Aurora. The enemy was mocking them, but the Lord used this experience to powerfully raise them up as skilled leaders and prayer ministers for the Kingdom.

Deliverance Is Integral

Deliverance is a ministry birthed in the heart of God. Like healing, it's part of His Kingdom reign. It's integral to His Kingdom message. When we love others in Jesus' name and trust in His authority to bring them to freedom, it gives Him joy and brings Him glory.

God tells us through the prophet Isaiah, "Is not this the kind of fasting I have chosen: to loose the chains of injustice and untie the cords of the yoke, to set the oppressed free and break every yoke?" (Isaiah 58:6). This has both social and spiritual applications that Jesus Himself modeled. Socially, He reached out to the poor and broken to "loose the chains of injustice." Spiritually, He cleared away the distractions of the enemy and brought us greater communion with the Father. "God anointed Jesus of Nazareth with the Holy Spirit and power. . . . He went around doing good and healing all who were under the power of the devil, because God was with him" (Acts 10:38). As philosopher and theologian Jacques Ellul put it, "Jesus Christ has conquered the world. He has stripped thrones, powers and dominions of their pretensions and of the autonomy. He is now and in actuality the Lord of the world and of history."[1]

Full training on deliverance ministry would need to be the scope of another book, but my point here is that setting people free from demonic oppression is a natural overflow of the Great Commission. As we preach the Good News and invite people to Christ, not only can they receive new life in Christ, but they can receive full salvation—they can be set free from the oppression of fear, sickness and evil spirits.

9 // Walking in Authority

(You Have More Than You Realize)

If we believe in a theology that doesn't contain doing
the works of Jesus, we will not have a practice of
Signs & Wonders . . .

—John Wimber

What it lies in our power to do, it lies in our power
not to do.

—Aristotle

I've tried to emphasize in these pages the significance of understanding the power that is deep-rooted in God's love for
us. We need to realize the huge importance of resisting the
spirit of fear in our lives, which keeps us battling accusation,
anxiety and a sense of disqualification. That power in His love
is there to help us resist fear and to give us the confidence to do
the stuff Jesus did. I hope you've arrived at this point feeling

encouraged, not overwhelmed or guilty. My goal is that each area of my teaching would bring not a sense of pressure or comparison, but a sense of the incredible freedom that is ours to walk in, which Paul describes this way:

> I also pray that you will understand the incredible greatness of God's power for us who believe him. This is the same mighty power that raised Christ from the dead and seated him in the place of honor at God's right hand in the heavenly realms. Now he is far above any ruler or authority or power or leader or anything else—not only in this world but also in the world to come. God has put all things under the authority of Christ and has made him head over all things for the benefit of the church. And the church is his body; it is made full and complete by Christ, who fills all things everywhere with himself.
>
> Ephesians 1:19–23 NLT

Over and over again throughout the prophets, the parables and the apostles' preaching, we see that God's heart is for us to know that we're sons and daughters who have been given free access to the rich and full inheritance of Christ. My belief is that one of the primary battles Satan wages is his attempt to keep us from a full revelation of that. Called *the Accuser*, he works to keep us in poverty when it comes to knowing God's love and walking in the authority God has given us. Satan wants us to keep our prayers in survival mode, focused on begging God for small withdrawals to cover our basic sustenance. He doesn't want us to realize that we've been entrusted with the Kingdom itself.

Adopting the elder brother's poverty mentality in the parable of the Prodigal Son actually keeps us alienated from all that the Father has for us (see Luke 15:11–32). Whereas the prodigal brother was kept in bondage by sin and shame, the elder brother was in bondage to a servant mentality. Neither son recognized the extent of their father's love—nor do we. The reality is that everything our Father has is ours. We are children who, through Christ, have come into an inheritance. Like any billionaire dad, our Father delights to see us working with the family bank account—investing, developing, causing the family's Kingdom to grow. In the past few years, my understanding of what's possible because of this has grown tremendously. We really do have more authority than we realize. And more authority than we are currently using.

Forthtelling in Times Square

It was rush hour in Times Square on a warm summer Saturday evening. The streets were a human spiderweb of sticky bodies pressed shoulder-to-shoulder from every continent of the world. I was there on vacation with my family. Clint Morgan, a Vineyard pastor friend of mine who lives in New York, had spent the day showing us around. It was about five o'clock in the afternoon. The streets and sidewalks were packed, and we were standing in the front of the M&M's World store.

Inside the store, I was gawking at the giant blue peanut Elvis M&M in the entrance, utterly amazed at the size of the thing. My wife, Angie, suddenly grabbed my arm and said, "Quick, tell me the phone number that appears on your phone."

I saw the incoming call on my phone and told her the number. Then I saw the older woman standing there with two security guards on walkie-talkies. Angie was really worked up as she repeated the number to the guards.

"What's going on?" I asked.

"This woman just lost her ten-year-old granddaughter," Angie told me. "She has no idea where the girl is, and she couldn't remember her own cell phone number to give to the security guards!"

I looked around at the thousands of people milling outside; this wasn't good.

The woman said, "I think I lost her four stores down, but I've been in every store and I can't find her anywhere. It's been a long time since I last saw her!"

The stores in Times Square are about the size of regular city blocks, and at this hour each one contained about the equivalent of a small Midwestern town. The reality of the situation hit the woman, and she burst into tears. Then came the clincher: "Our tour bus is about to leave for the airport in five minutes to catch our flight home. I don't know what to do!"

Sure enough, the buses were loading outside on the street. The situation was desperate.

I grabbed the woman's hand and asked, "Ma'am, do you believe in the power of prayer?"

She looked at me like *What?* but nodded. "Yeah, I think so. I've prayed before."

I asked her, "Do you believe God hears us when we pray?"

She replied, "I believe He does."

I told her, "I'm going to pray that your granddaughter will hear her name called out and that she'll be told to come here to the M&M's store—where her grandma is waiting in front of the blue Elvis M&M—in five minutes so that you'll know Jesus Christ loves you, is pursuing you and wants a personal relationship with you."

Then I prayed, "Father, in the name of Jesus, I thank You that You always hear me. I ask that You send someone or an angel to this granddaughter, wherever she is right now, and call her out by name. Tell her to leave where she's at, come immediately and stand in front of her grandmother in front of the giant blue Elvis M&M within three minutes, so that this woman will know that You're passionately pursuing her for a relationship and that You want to be involved in every part of her life. In Jesus' name, Amen."

I stood back and started counting, "One one-thousand, two one-thousand, three one-thousand . . ."

My pastor friend looked at me and asked, "Are you praying in tongues?" because he only saw my lips moving.

I said, "No, I'm counting."

By the time I counted to eighty-three one-thousand (about a minute and a half), the little girl came running in the door and called out, "Grandma!"

Still crying, the woman turned and grabbed her granddaughter and hugged her. Then she pushed her back and looked her in the face. "Where were you?" she asked. "How did you know where to find me?"

The little girl said, "I was four stores down, and I heard someone call me by name and say, 'Run to the M&M's candy store. Your grandmother is waiting for you there, in front of the blue Elvis M&M. Don't stop! Run now!' So I ran as fast as I could."

The grandmother spun back around and grabbed my hand. "I swear, I'll pray every day!" she said. "Every day, I'll pray!"

As they ran off to catch their bus, I shouted to her, "Never forget what Jesus did for you and that He's pursuing you and wants a relationship with you!"

She turned back to me and said, "How could I ever forget that after what just happened?"

My pastor friend turned to me in wonder and asked, "Did God tell you to pray that way?"

"No," I said.

His jaw dropped. "Then why did you?"

"Because if I didn't, nothing would've changed," I said.

Biblically I believe that we do have this kind of authority through Christ, though so much of it is still a mystery to me. But I stepped out to take a risk based more on what I believe than on what I had seen in the past. The more I've stepped out in faith and taken risks like that, the more I've realized the vast extent of the authority that is ours to walk in.

The Kingdom within You

John Wimber said this about the authority we walk in:

> Even though the Twelve were given authority & power of the Kingdom, they still had to exercise it. Until they actually healed the sick and cast out demons their power & authority meant little to them. To understand what you have you actually have to use it. And if you want more you have to give away what you've already been given.[1]

What happened that afternoon in New York is a demonstration of the real authority we carry in our words and actions to release things to happen in the natural. I call this kind of prophetic ministry "forthtelling," and I've seen it work for breakthrough, provision, healing and even for finding lost items or lost people. Forthtelling is speaking out to release things to happen for the benefit of others so that they will encounter God and see that He's real.

I believe forthtelling is the power and authority to actually release things to happen through our words. It's not so much anticipating what God is about to do, as it is God being in us, just as we are in Him. It's us acting directly out of the authority that God put within us when He said, "For in Christ lives all the fullness of God in a human body. So you also are complete through your union with Christ, who is the head over every ruler and authority" (Colossians 2:9–10 NLT).

I realize some prosperity teachers have abused and misused this authority. That's why many people stay away from such teaching and practice. The difference is that the abusers tried to use this authority for their own benefit and self-gain. This authority only works properly when we use it to benefit others and to accomplish the will of the Father to draw people into relationship with Himself. Jesus said that He "did not come to be served, but to serve" (Mark 10:45). That always has to stay at the heart of what we do in His name if we're to see the authority and power He has given us at work.

Under our new covenant through Christ, He has given us authority as heirs with Him to act and speak things into being that wouldn't otherwise occur (see Matthew 18:18). We can take authority over circumstances, breakthroughs, healing and even the weather. This stands in shocking contrast to the lies of Satan, the Accuser who seeks to belittle and disqualify us in every way. The ministry of Jesus is fully transferable to us, a principle that is firmly and consistently supported throughout all of Christ's teachings and His disciples' letters to the Church (see Luke 6:40; Romans 8:29; 2 Corinthians 3:18; Galatians 2:20; Colossians 3:9–10). As we walk in His footsteps, we're commissioned to extend the Kingdom of God. We see the demonstrable reality of the Kingdom break through as we walk in our God-given authority.

It's not magic. It's part of our inheritance, although our ability to walk in it is still imperfect. As Paul says in 1 Corinthians 13:12, now we see only see in part, we prophesy only in part. Not everything happens just the way we want it to, because the Kingdom of God is here, but still coming. Jesus submitted Himself to suffering in this world. He faced horrible persecution, He was unfairly tried for crimes He didn't commit and He even died on a cross. Yet wherever He went, He brought the breaking in of the Kingdom of God. In the tension and suffering and day-to-day life of paying taxes, being hungry and trudging through long, hot stretches of desert, He faithfully proclaimed the Kingdom.

Being a Kingdom people means that like Him, we live our lives in agreement with heaven, speaking and acting to accomplish what God wants to do here on earth (see Colossians 3:1–2). This life of ministry powerfully affirms our true identity in Christ, and it's extremely offensive to the "religious" and to the kingdom of darkness.

A Matter of Being

As we step out to minister with the authority we have in Christ, it's important to understand that just as He is one with the Father, we are one with Him. This is what Jesus said:

> Have I been with you so long, and yet you have not known Me . . . ? He who has seen Me has seen the Father; so how can you say, "Show us the Father"? Do you not believe that I am in the Father, and the Father in Me? The words that I speak to you I do not speak on My own authority; but the Father who dwells in Me does the works.
>
> John 14:9–10 NKJV

Because of fear, we don't understand the authority we have. Authority in the world is fear based. Authority in God is love based. First John 4:18 says, "The one who fears is not made perfect in love." Christ himself was not operating on earth as an all-powerful God, but rather, He operated on the authority that comes from God. To walk in godly authority means to walk under godly authority. The two are inseparable. Authority is not a matter of *doing*, it's a matter of *being*. It's about identity. Jesus asks that we "all may be one, as you, Father, are in Me, and I in You, that they also may be one in Us, that the world may believe that You sent me" (John 17:21 NKJV).

One definition of authority is "privilege and delegated influence." The Bible says that all authority on heaven and on earth has been given to Jesus, and that we have access to this power because He has transferred His ministry to us (see John 20:21–23). Another way to say this might be that we have access to *God* because Jesus has transferred His *relationship* to us. The Father-Son relationship falls within the very Being of God. It's the relationship through which "all things were made . . . without him nothing was made that was made" (John 1:3 NKJV). In the love of the Father and Son, we see that the oneness of God is the *relationship* of God, and all of life stems from it. In Jesus, God has drawn so near to man and drawn man so near to Himself that they are perfectly one. This is what the incarnation means.

Any first-year Sunday school child can tell you, "Jesus lives inside me." But have we really thought about what that means? It's not just that God will use us, but that He will actually live in us and through us. Incredibly, Jesus is fully God and fully human. Jesus has His Being by being one with the Father and the Holy Spirit. His oneness with God is the same oneness He extends to *us* through faith in Him, by the power of the Holy Spirit. Being born again means being born *into* God. Jesus said,

> And the glory which You gave Me I have given them, that they may be one just as We are one: I in them, and You in Me; that they may be made perfect in one, and that the world may know that You have sent Me, and have loved them as You have loved Me.
>
> John 17:22–23 NKJV

According to Thomas Torrance, former professor emeritus of Christian dogmatics at the University of Edinburgh,

> Being "in Christ" is not a sugary Christian metaphor—it's a riveting spiritual reality that should send shock waves down our spine, just as it sends demons screaming. It means that we actually share in the inner relations of God's own life and love. It means that the eternal communion of love in God overflows through Jesus Christ into our union with Christ and gathers us up to dwell with God and in God.[2]

This is crucial to understanding who we are in Christ. Both the Old and New Testaments are filled with depictions of God's people walking in tremendous authority. Christ releases and commissions all who believe in Him to go do what is in us. The more I've stepped out boldly on behalf of others in the name of Jesus, the more my ability to walk in His authority has grown. As Christians we believe in the miracles of Jesus, but do we actually believe God will be in us in the same way? Jesus said, "I tell you the truth, anyone who believes in me will do the same works I have done, and even greater works, because I am going to be with the Father" (John 14:12 NLT).

Sometimes we act as though Christ has set an unattainable bar that we must meekly edge toward from a million miles away. "But He's *Jesus*," we offer lamely.

"But *Jesus* is in *you*," the Bible offers back.

Comparing Christ's ministry with our ministry creates a false separation. All of it is His ministry in us. There's no glass ceiling on what that can look like. If we're kind, that's Him inside us. If He's kind—that's us. That's the nature He has placed inside us, and it's just waiting to get out!

Jesus came to set the standard of what's possible for a full-fleshed human being living in dependent relationship with God.

He then gave us His Spirit to reach that standard with. He didn't just give us an example or version 1.0, either. He gave us *Himself*. Do you really believe that the Spirit of the resurrected Christ lives inside you, or not? It's really better than sci-fi! Even a middle-of-the-pack believer has full authority to go out and do what Jesus did. (Personally, I'm just waiting for the day when we start dodging bullets *Matrix* style.) Why should we expect anything less than incredible?

Jesus the Mechanic and Wallet Finder?

One slushy Chicago winter day, I stopped to help a couple who had pulled over by the side of the road. I was in a hurry, and I asked them, "If I pray and your car starts right now, would you believe that it's Jesus telling you that He knows you and loves you?"

The couple looked at each other as if thinking, *This is a bit strange.* They were both shivering, though, and the guy clearly had been trying to get the engine going for a while. He looked at me and said, "If this car starts right now, it's definitely God!"

I put my hand on the engine and said, "In the name of Jesus, start." Then I told him, "Turn the key." The engine started right up.

Numerous times when people have lost their wallets or keys, I've asked them something similar and prayed. Within a few minutes or a few hours, the items have appeared in a place they couldn't have been before. I've told these stories all over the country, and people have tried the same sort of thing and have emailed me back many amazing stories of their own about how God acted as they stepped out and spoke in faith.

My dear friend Mike Smith, a principal in our area, recently called and told me a story that happened at his school. One of his teachers was desperately ransacking her desk and classroom, looking for some missing papers. He told her that he would pray and that God would put her papers in front of her. She looked at him strangely, but nodded. He prayed for the papers to come to the surface within the next ten minutes. As he turned to leave, she opened her top desk drawer—the one he had just watched her search through with no result—and the papers were sitting right there on top.

Kids don't have the same barriers we do about exercising our authority in Christ. The other day my son Elijah brought me his toy and said, "Daddy, the game's not working. Tell it to start working in the name of Jesus."

I hesitated but said, "Well, let's see if this works." It was an electronic game that wouldn't take the game card anymore. The card wouldn't stay in. I grabbed it and said, "In the name of Jesus, take the card and let the game stick."

Elijah pushed in the game, and it stuck. In his mind, of course that's what would happen. The game is part of creation just like everything else. He looked at me for a second, said, "Thank You, Jesus!" then grabbed the game and started playing. Honestly, I hadn't really been expecting anything to happen, but since my kid brought his request to me, I was like, "All right, let's do this." I think that's how God sees things, too, when His children make a request of Him.

Fully Transferable Ministry

In Ephesians 4, Paul writes, "Some of you—the apostles, prophets and pastors among you—have been given special gifts to be like Jesus and continue His ministry on earth. The rest of you, your job is just to concentrate on being nice."

Actually, come to think of it, that's not what Paul says at all. He writes that the whole role of leadership is to help equip and empower *every believer* to walk in the fullness of Christ's ministry. He defines leaders this way:

> Their responsibility is to equip God's people to do his work and build up the church, the body of Christ. This will continue until we all come to such unity in our faith and knowledge of God's Son that we will be mature in the Lord, measuring up to the *full and complete* standard of Christ.
>
> Ephesians 4:11–13 NLT, emphasis added

Paul also writes in Galatians 4:19, "Oh, my dear children! I feel as if I'm going through labor pains for you again, and they will continue until Christ is fully developed in your lives." That shows that Christ's life and ministry is not for the elite few! The hierarchy and classism in the Church was the result of syncretism—the blending together of the Church and the pagan religions of Rome under Constantine. When Rome stopped persecuting the growing body of Christians, the Romans decided to co-opt Christianity into their society. They appointed Roman nobles as "leaders" of the Church and gave them aristocratic robes to wear, which is what High Church bishops wear today.

That seems a reverse of the upside-down Kingdom Christ established, in which the humble are exalted and the exalted are humbled. Scripture tells us that we have one Father in heaven (see Matthew 23:9) and one standard to achieve—that of Christ. Through the Spirit, each of us has the potential to measure up to the full and complete standard of Christ—in purity, gentleness, power and wisdom. The risen Christ is now glorified beyond measure, but His Spirit lives in us to perfect in us His life here on earth in His suffering, in His miracles, in His love.

Don't Fake Being Authentic

Our world screams for authenticity. Christ *in* you is the hope of glory. If you're not bringing Christ to the world, you might as well stay home. But don't worry—you are bringing Him! "For God wanted them [His people] to know that the riches and glory of Christ are for you Gentiles, too. And this is the secret: Christ lives in you" (Colossians 1:27 NLT).

This was God's plan all along, yet as Christians we're confused about our role. We think we should be *like* Jesus, and strangely, most of our interpretation of that revolves around being nice. We think of Christlikeness as being more like Mother Teresa or Grandma. It's exhausting, it's discouraging, and we fail at it.

Why not think of Christlikeness more as being like William Wallace in *Braveheart*? Because if it's about being sweet and nice, then how in the world are we going to even think about doing the things Jesus did? And if you think doing the things Jesus did was hard, try being perfect. Matthew 5:48 tells us to be perfect, as our Father in heaven is perfect. Yet only God is perfect. We're not invited to be *like* Christ so much as actually to be *in* Christ. This is not meant to overwhelm us, but to encourage us.

Apart from God we can't do anything anyway, so we can stop trying. Stop it! Stop trying, and let God. God's plan was not that some people would encounter God and everybody else would just hear about it secondhand or thirdhand from that kid who always got straight A's in class. God's plan was that people would meet Christ themselves, in you and me.

Newsflash of the day: "Christians trying to be like God" are not the hope of the world. It's Christ *in* us that's the hope of glory.

What if you really knew that your only job was to love and receive love from God? The love of the Father isn't simply a flawless attribute to be imperfectly imitated; it's a relationship of perfect intimacy that you're invited to fully experience. God wants absolutely nothing less than to fill you with Himself and make you *shine* with His presence through the Holy Spirit. Jesus said, "I tell you the truth: It is for your good that I am going away. Unless I go away, the Counselor will not come to you; but if I go, I will send him to you" (John 16:7 NIV1984).

A friend of mine, the one and only Bill Johnson, pastor of Bethel Church in Redding, California, says that the Holy Spirit is trapped inside unbelieving believers, and He wants out. Bill doesn't say this harshly, but as a word of hope. It's a word of childlikeness, too. What if we knew that everything we need, and more than we could possibly imagine or hope for, actually lives inside us? It's also a word of rest. The only thing we should be striving for is to rest in the reality of God with us. Jesus' very name, Emmanuel, actually means "God with us." Union with God is the most powerful thing about us—it's who we are. And we should expect greatness. Expecting that we were made for greatness is also childlike. Don't let anyone take that expectation away from you.

Dominion Rule

The "Kingdom of God" is translated in the New Testament from the Greek word *basileia*, which means "dominion rule." Minister and theologian George Ladd mentioned that the "kingdom of God is the sovereign rule of God, manifested in the person and work of Christ, creating a people over whom he reigns, and issuing in a realm or realms in which the power of his reign is realized."[3] The dominion rule of God is the restoration of that love relationship that transforms everything it touches. Christ came as the new Adam:

> The first man Adam became a living being; the last Adam, a life-giving spirit. The spiritual did not come first, but the natural, and after that the spiritual. The first man was of the dust of the earth; the second man is of heaven. As was the earthly man, so are those who are of the earth; and as is the heavenly man, so also are those who are of heaven. And just as we have borne the image of the earthly man, so shall we bear the image of the heavenly man.
>
> 1 Corinthians 15:45–49

Much of current dominion theology has messed up this concept. I'm not talking about a political system in which Christians try to take over the government. Jesus didn't go there. What He did through His perfect life and death on the cross was to restore back to humanity the original authority over the earth that God gave us in the Garden. He made us the bearers of heaven. By renouncing sin and declaring Christ as Lord, we receive the gift of His Spirit and His Kingdom reign within us. He has called us as co-heirs to the Kingdom and has thus granted us full authority to choose, just as He freely chose.

The Kingdom of Heaven is within us. As we submit our lives to Christ, His Kingdom reigns in us. It's at once as supernatural as it is organic. We've been given a fully Holy Spirit into our fully human bodies—His realm must extend fully through each part of our mind, will, heart, emotions, attitudes, relationships, hobbies, spending, passions and habits, until we perfectly reflect God's glory. It's a process of sanctification that touches every part of who we are. Jesus died not only because of our sins, but because we fell short of the glory of God. In fact, the more literal Greek translation of the phrase "fall short of the glory of God" is that we gave it up. We were supposed to be carrying the *glory* that was assigned to God, and we surrendered it in the Garden because of unbelief.

Satan is still trying to keep us from God's glory through unbelief. He whispers, "Who do you think you are? You can't do that! You'll fail and hurt the Gospel if you try." Satan ministers fear to us, and we think it's our own thought process and fall for it. Jesus died to bring us back to the glory we fell short of; He brings us into royal priesthood. Priesthood was modeled in the Old Testament by those who were qualified to enter into the Holy of Holies, encounter the Father God and act on behalf of the community. The Holy Spirit makes possible today that kind of intimate communion with the Father, and everything we receive from Him, we can give away. We carry His presence with us, and from that flows our ministry in this world.

To walk in authority is to be a carrier of this transforming presence. As we abide in Him and He abides in us, we should expect nothing less than the reordering of ourselves and our world according to this perfect love relationship. This is what it means to declare the Kingdom of God. When Jesus was asked, "Are you the one who is to come, or should we expect someone else?" He replied, "Go back and report to John what you have seen and heard: The blind receive sight, the lame walk, those who have leprosy are cleansed, the deaf hear, the dead are raised, and the good news is proclaimed to the poor" (Luke 7:20, 22). To do the things that Jesus did is to walk in the authority of His name, "God with us." Torrance wrote this about the name of Christ:

> To pronounce the name of Jesus Christ means to acknowledge that we are cared for, that we are not lost. Jesus Christ is man's

salvation in all circumstances and in [the] face of all that darkens his life, including the evil that proceeds from himself. . . . The Kingdom of Heaven does exist already; from God's side action has been already taken for our good. . . . There is nothing which is not already made good in this happening, that God became man for our good. Anything that is left can be no more than the discovery of this fact. We do not exist in any kind of gloomy uncertainty; we exist through the God who was gracious to us before we existed at all.[4]

How do we live that out? How do we demonstrate that we actually believe God will work through us? We do it through praying, ministering, speaking and acting. There's not a situation in the world God can't break in to. The missing ingredient isn't God; He's done His part. The missing ingredient is us. As I said earlier, when we walk into a situation as carriers of His presence and authority, God is there because we are there. He shows up because we've shown up and He's in us—Christ in us, the hope of the world. This doesn't mean that we never doubt, but where we let our actions exceed our doubts, that's faith. Since God says to abide in Him and He'll abide in us, should we expect anything less than the authority to route demons, raise the dead, heal the sick or for that matter, stop traffic in Times Square?

A Man under Authority

As He journeyed through different towns and proclaimed the Gospel, Jesus was amazed to discover along the way a man who understood authority. A centurion approached Jesus and asked for a healing for his servant. Jesus agreed to come with him, but the man stopped Him, saying,

Lord, I am not worthy that you should come under my roof. But only speak a word, and my servant will be healed. For I also am a man under authority, having soldiers under me. And I say to this one, "Go," and he goes; and to another, "Come," and he comes; and to my servant, "Do this," and he does it.

Matthew 8:8–9 NKJV

Interestingly, the centurion didn't identify himself to Jesus as a man who *had* authority, but rather as one who was *under* authority. The soldiers that submitted to him did so because he was under the delegated authority of Caesar and the Roman Empire. The centurion demonstrated that he rightly understood the source of Jesus' authority as not being from within Himself, but from God. Christ's authority came from a life that was fully authorized by God with power. Jesus was amazed at the man's understanding and praised his faith, saying it was greater than any He had seen in all of Israel.

Our ability to walk in authority hinges on our ability to recognize and walk *under* the Father's authority. Jesus taught His followers,

If anyone's will is to do God's will, he will know whether the teaching is from God or whether I am speaking on my own authority. The one who speaks on his own authority seeks his own glory; but the one who seeks the glory of him who sent him is true, and in him there is no falsehood.

John 7:17–18 ESV

During the cool of the day, that special time that Adam and Eve spent in the Garden with the Father, I believe a sync of "wills" occurred. Likewise, a sync of wills occurred when Jesus pulled away from the crowds to spend time with His Father. Spending time with the Father, we can follow the stirring that's in our hearts to do something, because we've been with Him and we're operating with His heart and within His will.

God's authority brings blessing, and honoring the God-given authority on someone's life allows God to bless us through that person. That's what happened when the centurion honored the God-given authority of Jesus. Those who recognized and submitted to the authority Jesus walked in were able to receive great miracles through Him. The woman who was bleeding for twelve years didn't ask Jesus to heal her. She recognized the authority He walked in, and by simply touching the hem of His garment she came under that authority. Jesus felt the power go out from Him and even asked who had touched Him. The woman had appealed to God through the authority that rested on Jesus, and she received a miracle from God by recognizing the impartation that rested on Him (see Luke 8:42–48).

Jesus also taught that "Anyone who receives a prophet because he is a prophet will receive a prophet's reward, and anyone who receives a righteous man because he is a righteous man will receive a righteous man's reward" (Matthew 10:41 niv1984). The prophet walks in delegated authority on behalf of God and receives a reward for submitting to the authority of God's message. Likewise, the person who correctly recognizes the source of the prophet's authority as being God is submitting to the same delegation and is equally rewarded. A righteous man submits to God's authority given through His Word and receives a reward for it. The man who simply recognizes the authority of God's Word as lived out in the life of the righteous man receives the same reward!

The issue of authority is powerfully recognized throughout Scripture and in the life of Jesus. We must equally appreciate its importance in our lives. Recognized authority and mutual submission flow from the inner workings of the Trinity and are integral to our spiritual growth and sonship. In the same high degree that blessing flows through God's authority, attitudes of rebellion and discord in our lives open us up to demonic influence and give the prince of rebellion a foothold in our lives, relationships and ministry.

Rooted and Grounded in Love

When it comes to leadership and spiritual authority, one of the most important qualifications is a deep, deep sense of the knowledge of God's love for us. Our authority comes from the love of the Father toward the Son, which has been passed on to us through Christ's death and resurrected life. Our revelation of the Father's love (which is different from knowledge about it) is what allows the fullness of God to dwell in us. This is the principle of abiding, in which Christ says that if we will abide in Him, He will abide in us (see John 15:4). Paul also gave us an incredible picture in Ephesians 3:14–19 (ESV) of the significance of God's love for His people and all that His love does for us:

> For this reason I bow my knees before the Father, from whom every family in heaven and on earth is named, that according to the riches of his glory he may grant you to be strengthened with power through his Spirit in your inner being, so that Christ may dwell in your hearts through faith—that you, being rooted and grounded in love, may have strength to comprehend with all the saints what is the breadth and length and height and depth, and to know the love of Christ that surpasses knowledge, that you may be filled with all the fullness of God.

It's possible to have faith to heal the sick but still be living in condemnation. Without a revelation of the Father's love, our many good works or wonderful giftings become like a clanging gong that has a wincing effect on the people around us.

Authority that comes from abiding in Christ allows us to minister out of a sense of the generosity of God's love. When leadership doesn't come from this overflow of having our needs met in God, there's a constant temptation to use power and authority to fill our needs. We also try to gain a sense of worth that mistakenly comes from dominating or controlling others. Insecurity and pride are two things that set themselves up against walking in godly authority. One worships our lack as the defining thing about us; the other exalts God's goodness in our lives as being our own goodness. When we don't look to God to meet our needs, we become insecure and dependent on those we wish to serve, looking to them to provide us with a sense of affirmation and to keep our painful sense of inadequacy from hurting.

When we allow God to meet our needs, though, He gives us the gift of being able to serve others from a place of freedom. Bringing our insecurity to God for healing sets us free, and repenting of pride allows Him to empower us with His grace. God opposes the proud, but gives grace to the humble (see James 4:6).

Because of Moses' humility, God spoke to him face-to-face and appointed him as the first authority over his people (see Numbers 12:3–8). "For the eyes of the LORD range throughout the earth to strengthen those whose hearts are fully committed to him" (2 Chronicles 16:9). As we seek to posture our hearts correctly toward God, His love and authority increasingly flow in our lives.

10 // Wounded Healers?

Hope to a Hurting World

Although the world is full of suffering, it is also full of the overcoming of it.

—Helen Keller

I would rather live in a world where my life is surrounded by mystery than live in a world so small that my mind could comprehend it.

—Harry Emerson Fosdick

In the film *Furious Love*, I talk about a dream I had eighteen years ago where I was sitting in a church sanctuary filled with about eight hundred people. As I looked around, I realized that everybody was doing messed-up things. People were having sex in the pews. Gangsters were fighting in the church. Prostitutes were soliciting business, and people were doing drugs and screaming at each other. In my vision, I was running around trying to stop it all. I kept yelling at everyone, "You have to stop! If you aren't going to honor God's house, then get out now! This can't be happening here!"

The Lord was standing next to me as I was working to get everybody to stop. He asked me, "Why would you send away what I've sent in? Why would you send away the very thing you've been asking for?"

Shocked, I looked at Him. "God, I didn't ask for this!"

"You asked Me for the lost. Now here they are," He said. "I want *you* to leave."

I was shocked again. "God, You're telling *me* to leave? I'm a pastor here—I'm Your guy. How can You tell me to leave?"

"Leave now," He said.

As I stepped out of the church door, everything disappeared and my feet crunched on gravel. In front of me was a set of train tracks, and lying across the tracks was an older, gray-haired gentleman who was very well dressed. To the right of us was an old train station, and as I looked down the tracks, I saw a massive train coming in the distance.

I thought, *I've got to get this guy off the tracks or he'll be crushed and killed!* I started trying to drag him off, and I kept telling him, "Get up, get up! You've got to move—you've got to get off the tracks!"

It was impossible to move the man. It was as if he were alive, but lifeless.

"No, this is where I belong," he told me.

I was so worried for him, but finally the Lord stopped me and said, "Don't worry about the man on the tracks; worry about getting on that train. This train is coming, and I want you on it."

About then the train arrived, and I jumped back from the tracks. The train went over the man and crushed him. As soon as that happened, I didn't care about him anymore. It was done. (I have a feeling this man represented the old way of doing things that would obstruct the new, but I'm not totally sure—the meaning may still be unfolding.)

I looked at the side of the train, and it said, "*MOVE OF GOD.*" I reached out with both hands and grabbed on to the side. The train was *flying* through the air at tremendous speed, and I was flying through the air with it, trying to hang on. Finally I pulled myself into the door. When I stepped inside the train, I was stepping back into the sanctuary in front of all those people whom I had just left. They were still doing all those terrible things in church.

Confused and dismayed, I said, "This is the train? This is a move of God?"

The Lord spoke to me again and said, "Now keep it simple. Love them. Let Me change them. I just want you to bring Me into the mix. Don't focus on their wrongs."

In my dream, I began to present the Gospel to those people in as simple a form as I knew how. All around the sanctuary, they quieted down and started listening. Then I said, "If you want what I just described, come forward."

The response was like a tidal wave of people. They were running and crawling over the top of each other and screaming out, "*I have to have this!*" Drug dealers were pulling money out of their pockets and saying, "I'll give you everything if I can have what you're talking about."

All around the room, people were crying out because they so badly wanted what I'd presented. Overwhelmed with emotion, I dropped to the ground in the dream and began to cry.

Suddenly, I saw a cloud form in the ceiling of that sanctuary. Lightning bolts were shooting across the cloud, and the Lord spoke to me and said, "Call down the cloud."

It was a cloud of His presence. I called for the cloud to rest on the people. Within the cloud, lightning bolts began surging through the people. Incredibly, as I watched, I saw people rise up in this cloud, and then as soon as the cloud lifted, the people bolted out the church door. I thought, *Well, it came and it went.*

But then all the people who went out brought other people back in and prayed for them. People were being healed; people were being transformed. It was happening all over the room, everywhere I looked. I dropped to my knees and began to weep in my dream, saying, "God, I don't know what this is, but this *has* to happen. Whatever this is, this is what the Church is supposed to look like. Let this happen." Then I woke up weeping.

His Kindness Makes Us Great

Jesus said, "Those who are well have no need of a physician, but those who are sick. I came not to call the righteous, but sinners" (Mark 2:17 ESV). We live in a world of sin and suffering, and it disturbs us. It breaks our hearts. Yet if God got rid of sin in the world, none of us would be left in it. Instead, He chose to rebuild from within. The Bible repeatedly shows that God's purpose is accomplished in the midst of brokenness by people who are not "qualified" by any stretch of the imagination to be used by Him. Jacob was a cheater; Peter had a temper; David had an affair; Noah got drunk; Jonah ran from God; Rahab was a prostitute; Paul was a murderer; Gideon was insecure; Miriam was a gossiper; Martha was a worrier; Thomas was a doubter; Sara was impatient; Elijah was moody; Moses stuttered; Zacchaeus was short; Abraham was old and Lazarus was dead. Yet all these people are listed as friends of God and were used for His purposes. They were even listed in His "Faith Hall of Fame" (see Hebrews 11).

The cross lets us scorn shame and pain and sin. The devil wants to name us by our sin so he can get us to sin again. Grace comes along and says, "You're too awesome to act like that! This isn't who you really are. Girl, get up out of that mud and dust off that white dress. You're a princess—ride with Me into the Kingdom to do My work at My side. Son, rise up! I've called you by name and chosen you for My purpose. Come with Me, My son, and let Me show you the secrets of My Kingdom."

What prevents us from having that kind of intimacy with God? Many of us hold God at a distance because we don't realize how afraid of Him we are. We act out of an Old Covenant understanding. In Exodus, look what the people did when they saw God at a distance:

> The people were afraid and trembled, and they stood far off and said to Moses, "You speak to us, and we will listen; but do not let God speak to us, lest we die." Moses said to the people, "Do not fear. . . ." The people stood far off, while Moses drew near to the thick darkness where God was.
>
> Exodus 20:18–21 ESV

The people didn't understand God, but then Jesus came as the exact representation of God so that people might know God and have life (see John 10:10; 14:9; Hebrews 1:3). God's Word says, "He who fears has not been made perfect in love" (1 John 4:18 NKJV).

We have such a fear of failure and rejection, and we allow the imperfect authority figures we encounter in our lives to define our view of God. Human authority is often marked by punishment and the use of fear to exhibit power over others. God is the only being in the universe who has never been marked by insecurity in any way. Authority is not the mark of His personality; He has no need for it and has rarely exhibited it in His relations with man. Scripture gives us one picture of this in the prophet Elijah's encounter with God in the cave (see 1 Kings 19). God was not in the fire, the wind or the storm. He came as a still, gentle whisper, which His friend Elijah immediately recognized.

King David, one of God's closest friends in the Bible and the greatest king to rule over Israel, wrote, "Your gentleness makes me great" (Psalm 18:35 NASB). We can be set free from defending ourselves or fighting our own battles by knowing God's gentleness and fierce love. God longs for us to recognize His loyalty to us in every situation we encounter. Our long journeys in the "wilderness" or into seasons of "captivity" are often lengthened until we recognize God's loving provision over our lives. This was profoundly illustrated in the Israelites' forty-year journey to the Promised Land and their seventy-year exile and captivity in Babylon.

Even in our worst rebellion, God says to us, "All day long I have held out my hands to an obstinate people . . . a people who continually provoke me to my very face" (Isaiah 65:2–3). When we don't recognize His love, we remain stuck in a slavery mentality and obstinately become not only the greatest hazard to ourselves, but the greatest obstacle to the good that God intends.

Beauty for Ashes

God pursues our hearts. He knows our hurts, and that's where He chooses to love us first. Jesus washed His disciples' feet, knowing what they had walked through. He had been with them the whole day, and He knew where their feet had been. He knew what they would smell like, and that it wouldn't be nice.

The prophets foresaw beauty for ashes and garments of praise replacing black mourning clothes (see Isaiah 61). The Kingdom message is about such exchanges—the poor hearing the Good News, the walking dead becoming alive for the first time. It's about a dry, dry army of bones being given muscles and tendons and flesh, as in Ezekiel's vision, so that they can feel again. Their hearts will beat with love once more, and the breath of life in them brings hope, and with it, a battle cry.

Once I tasted this and saw it, and once I understood the Kingdom message—that such exchanges are not just the icing on the cake, but that the blind seeing and the lame walking are literally and figuratively the meat and message of the Kingdom—I realized that there was so much more I had to have. This was the place I had to live in. Every one of us can have the same testimony as the blind man Jesus healed who said, "I was blind but now I see" (John 9:25 NASB).

If you don't get that, you won't get the Kingdom. Each of us is crippled in our own way. It's Jesus who reaches down, takes us by the hand and says, "Walk." Even with our shrunken, twisted legs still hanging limp beneath us, we're told, "Get up and walk." It might even seem cruel, but this is grace. Grace is the power of God to do the will of God. In the Kingdom clash between the "already" and the "not yet," we are wounded healers, His message of hope to a hurting world. God in us is the hope of glory. We still go out and give words when we need words ourselves. We're still used by God to bring healing, comfort, wholeness and restoration to others when we're sick, weak and weary ourselves.

For some of us, the breakthrough revelation is that God loves *others* so much that He's even willing to use *us* to reach them. It's simple. We can get caught up thinking that we have to wait until we are holy enough or anointed enough, and then God will use us, or we can realize that we are told to go—go now.

As you and I step into obedience and go, the process itself will refine us, stretch us and strengthen us. Most of the time, God will call us to go just outside of our comfort zone. Living in that place of risk and dependency on God is throwing ourselves on His mercy; He will both build us up and tear down what needs to go. Listen, learn, grow, take risks. It's fun. There is incredible pleasure in seeing God work and in collaborating with the Holy Spirit in everyday life. We serve the one true God, and stepping out to do Kingdom things is like having a front row seat. It's not that *we* have to be amazing; it's that *He* is amazing. That's the power of our testimony—that God would use broken, hurt, wounded, messed-up people like us. That's part of the Gospel message. The disciples went before the rulers of their age, and the rulers' reaction was, "These guys *must* have been with Jesus!" God's power in the disciples was that obvious, though it was also still obvious that they were simple fishermen with no education. They were simple men who walked and talked with God, just as we are.

My testimony as Robby Dawkins is that if God can use me, He can use anybody. The invitation of God is for us to step out. This is what it means to be living epistles. God doesn't call the qualified; He qualifies the called. The fact that God would use you and me *screams* hope to the world.

"Jesus, Heal Me"

My son Canah was diagnosed with autism when he was two years old. Up until the age of nine months, he seemed completely normal. As he got older, his behavior deteriorated into that of someone far younger than his age. He lost the few words he'd learned, and then it seemed as though he shut down and went backward.

When Canah was diagnosed, I remember the sinking feeling that came over me when I heard. The doctor basically told us that we should prepare to take care of him for the rest of his life. Canah was one of the most severe cases of autism he had ever seen. He warned us that Canah would probably never speak and that he would never function normally. I didn't see Angie show much sadness. The defensive mother in her rose up like a hawk. The look in her eyes at the doctor was, *I'm going to make you eat those words.* I think she said something out loud like, "We'll see about that."

I was stunned. I remember going back home and starting to pray for Canah every morning and every night. I would put my hand on his chest and say, "Jesus, heal Canah." I did this for years; I still do.

One night when I came in to pray for him, he said the first sentence I'd ever heard come out of his mouth. When I put my hand on his chest, he closed his eyes and said, "Jesus, heal me." It sent chills down my spine. I remember thinking, *What could get the attention of God more than an autistic boy crying out to be restored?*

After that, I kept praying and praying. When Canah started preschool, there were three different classes: severe, moderate and high functioning. He started at the bottom of the severe category. Within four months, the teachers met with us and said, "We're amazed at what we're seeing; he's completely blowing us away! We want to move him to the top of the class."

We were elated. By the end of the year, he had moved to the bottom of the moderate class. By the end of the next year, they put him at the top. When he started the year after that (in five-year-old kindergarten), he went to the bottom of the high-functioning class. Again, within a few months he was at the top of his class. When he started elementary school, Angie was able to get him into a regular classroom with an aide.

I believe this was God healing him, and I also want to honor the dozens of hardworking teachers, friends and therapists who loved him, helped him and prayed for him along the journey. We kept praying, "Lord, open the doors that we need."

Angie says I was in denial about Canah. I don't remember ever shedding a tear over his condition. I just remember saying, "Okay, this is our new challenge. We'll figure out how to make this work. This is our next mountain to climb. People deal with this all the time." When I prayed for Canah for healing, it was never, "God, would You smile down on us and take away the autism?" My attitude was, *God has a plan for this child, too, and we're not going to let this rob him. Now, I curse autism and its effects on my child.*

Canah has a special grace on his life. We had been so worried about his behavior causing problems for teachers and distracting other kids in class, but actually he was always the favorite. I remember different teachers buying him special gifts. We almost became concerned about the favoritism they showed him!

We've had people give us prophetic words that by the time Canah gets to junior high, he'll be completely "normal." Of course we hold on to that, but at the same time it doesn't change our course with him. Either way, this is a life that God has created. The enemy doesn't want that life to be fully functional. We're not going to take that sitting down, so we are raising a wounded healer.

Big Guns

Over the past few years, Canah has prayed for many people and has seen them healed. In my mind, this is what it means to be a living temple. Yes, outwardly we struggle, we're imperfect, we're wounded—but God chose to live inside us and carry out His plan of salvation in the world.

One time Angie and Canah (then age seven) came with me to a conference in Iowa. I was standing in front of eight hundred people, praying for a girl with scoliosis. She was in a lot of pain, and her spine had a severe curvature. I prayed several times, and the pain went down to a level 6 and then just stayed there. All of a sudden I got the sense that I needed to bring Canah up.

I had already told the story of Canah's autism at this conference and how God had worked through it. I said, "Canah, come here; run to Daddy. I need a big gun up here." He came running up next to me, and I said, "Hey, Canah, pray for this girl."

Canah put his hand on her back and said, "Back, go straight. Pain, you get out right now."

The girl lunged forward, and her back started moving. You could hear the vertebrae popping. When it stopped, you could see that her back was perfectly straight. Before that, her shoulders had been all twisted and hunched.

The girl stood up straight and said, "All the pain is gone!"

Using wounded healers like Canah to heal others is one way God gets revenge against the kingdom of darkness. A highly dysfunctional boy who was never supposed to speak prayed for someone else. He spoke out, breaking the power of sickness and suffering, and a girl found healing and freedom from pain. My son is a picture of God's love and a picture of hope for the world.

If you have thoughts like, *I'm too broken; I'm too sick; I haven't been healed myself; I have issues*, then you're missing the point. Using wounded healers is how God strikes back.

Resist Discouragement

Hudson Taylor, one of the first missionaries to China, faced incredible obstacles—sickness, stoning and being near death. He described lying in bed for months with terrible depression. Then he wrote that everything changed for him one year when he realized that he was supposed to resist discouragement the same way that we resist sin.

Discouragement is not a natural emotion we simply cycle through. It's one of the only ones Scripture consistently commands us to resist: "Be strong and courageous. Do not be afraid; do not be discouraged, for the LORD your God will be with you wherever you go" (Joshua 1:9). With every battle you face, the biggest thing I would say is stick with it. Keep praying. Don't give up. Continue to contend. You've got to make the commitment that you won't get discouraged. Declare, "I'm going to pray, but I'm not going to get discouraged. I'm not going to get disillusioned and think that God doesn't love me." As a Kingdom people, we have to determine that that will be our resolution. All of us will face obstacles at one time or another that seem insurmountable. It takes resolve to say, "If I get into praying for people and prophesying for people, I'm not going to get discouraged or disillusioned."

The results of what we do are for the Lord, as I've said, not for us. You and I don't have any right to think, *Why didn't God hear me when I prayed?* In any situation, there are natural factors to deal with, and then there is also the spiritual side of things. Our problem is not other people or God refusing to heal. He has already given us everything we need—He has given us Himself. Our battle is against the spiritual powers of the dark world and the spiritual forces of evil in the heavenly realm (see Ephesians 6:12). We're involved in a battleground and we're all wounded soldiers, so don't be discouraged by the difficulties you see in yourself or in your circumstances. In difficult times, don't feel as if you've missed it or God has forgotten you. He hasn't, not ever.

Fighting Cancer with Mom

My mom was diagnosed with colon cancer. I'll never forget the day my dad called to tell me the news. He said, "Your mom . . ." and then kept choking up every time he tried to get it out. When I heard him break down like that, I thought she had died. I started freaking out, hollering, "Dad, no, no, no!"

Then finally he got the words out. "I don't think you understood. She has cancer."

We went to Atlanta for Mom's surgery. It was really bad. The doctors said, "We're not sure this will take care of all of it; we may need to do some other things." While it appeared that the cancer was gone, they said the slightest little cell that remained could cause more cancer to develop.

We prayed about it, and we had peace. We thought things would be okay. Mom was fine for a while, and it seemed as though the surgery had been successful. As time went on, though, the cancer came back. We were devastated. We started praying again, and the Lord spoke very clearly to me that this time it was unto death. I had never had any kind of word like that before, so I was really concerned. I battled within, wondering if I should tell my dad. I didn't know how to handle it. After a few days, I worked up the courage to share with my dad what the Lord had shown me. My dad said he was going to keep praying no matter what.

I flew my parents up to Chicago so we could help take care of my mom. Slowly, we watched horrific pain come into her body.

At times, she was screaming out in horrible pain. One night I heard my dad in her room. He was crying out at the top of his lungs for his wife's life for hours. The whole time, I knew in my heart that she was going to go.

Here was this wrenching picture of a man fighting for the life of his wife. It was such an incredible picture of love. Dad served her hand and foot, tenderly caring for her and loving her no matter what. It was what she needed. For the most private things, Mom would allow only Dad to take care of her. The rest of us were taking care of him so that he could help her.

We finally had to take Mom to the hospital. My father was sobbing, saying, "We're going to fight this!"

I resolved with him, "Okay, if you want to fight, we're with you. We're going to fight this." My sisters and our families filled Mom's hospital room with worship and prayer for her.

One night as we were worshiping, a woman from the room next door came and asked us if we would visit her sister, who had cancer in her kidney. She said, "We're not Christians, but would you just come and sing one of your songs with her?"

My dad and my uncle are both pastors, and they said, "Hey, let's go pray for her." Her name was Violet Kindle. She was lying in bed in the last stages of kidney cancer. She had been catheterized, and the bag hanging by her bed was supposed to be full of urine, but it was full of blood. We started praying for her, not necessarily for healing, but for comfort and peace. I felt the Lord clearly speak to me and say, "Tell her I'm healing her body of cancer."

I told Violet that God was healing her of cancer. At first it felt as if I had sawdust in my mouth, and the words stuck in my throat. Then they came out flat. My mom, this missionary and Bible teacher who had sacrificed her whole life for others—the most godly person I've ever known in my life—was dying in the room next door.

But I looked at this woman and told her, "Not only is God taking away all the cancer right now, but there's also a family member who's giving you a big problem. God will completely resolve it by the end of the day." Then I said, "I gotta go!" I was just so overwhelmed by this message from the Lord for Violet, and part of me was also wondering, *Lord, how could You do that? My mom has been a faithful servant, unlike Violet (a "heathen"). Yet You would completely heal Violet and let my mom die?* I went back to my mom's room, where it seemed as though nothing was resolved.

A few hours passed, and Violet's sister came running back into Mom's room from next door. "Hey, you gotta see this!" she said, and she showed us Violet's catheter bag. All the blood was gone; it contained only urine.

I asked, "They changed the bag?"

"No," she said, "it's been the same bag the whole time I've been sitting here. The oncologist is on the way."

The next morning when we went to see Mom, I saw Violet's sister standing down the hall, bouncing up and down. She said, "I'm so glad you're here. I've been waiting for you this whole time. The oncologist is in there with my sister now."

We went in and the doctor was standing there looking at Violet's chart and saying, "I can't believe it! I really can't believe it—all the cancer's gone!"

After he left we talked to Violet, and she reminded me of what I had prayed yesterday. She said, "What you mentioned about my family has been a big problem for me. My son-in-law has been living with me, but he divorced my daughter. She left a while back, but I couldn't get him to leave. Yesterday he called and said, 'Okay, okay, I'm moving out.' I asked him what he meant, and he said, 'Those guys you sent over here—tell them I'm moving out.'"

She looked at me and asked, "Did you send some guys over to my apartment?"

I shook my head, "Of course not. I don't even know where you live." But God had taken care of things His way.

Both Violet and her sister ended up coming to Christ. Mom passed away a short time later, and they were present at her funeral. I looked over the lid of my mom's coffin at these two women whom the Lord had saved, one of whom He also healed, and I understood that Mom being in the hospital at the same time that God gave these two women an opportunity to come to Christ was His mercy for them.

Fight for It

When we talk about living with sin and suffering in the world, I don't believe the "suck it up" mentality is scriptural. It will not last you long. It's not about gritting your teeth, tightening your belt and saying, "This is God's will for my life." When we're in that place of suffering, we need to take after the woman who bled for twelve years. She put herself right in the middle of where Jesus was, and I believe she had to fight for it, with the crowd pushing against her and her feelings of shame at being an outcast dragging her down. Labeled "unclean," think of the sense of rejection she must have battled just to touch the hem of His garment. She risked public humiliation, scorn and even punishment. She is the picture of perseverance and resolve to seek after Jesus, His presence and His Kingdom in the midst of suffering and desperation.

All of us will face issues in our lives that will make us want to hit the eject button and isolate ourselves in our pain. Then off by ourselves, we build our theology around our disappointment to console ourselves. Somehow we have to resolve that when that happens, we will not stop clinging to Jesus. He is ever present with us, our hiding place and Rock. In every situation of suffering I've encountered, God has been there every time when I've turned to Him. Instead of turning to Him, however, it's easy to allow anger, bitterness or unforgiveness to become our shelter. Those create a thick wall of defense against the outside world, but they also become our private prisons where we can live in the regret of our past mistakes, rehearsing them over and over again and letting them bring us to a halt. I think of the prophet Samuel, who mourned and grieved over King Saul and the disappointment of what had been lost. God's word to Samuel was, "How long will you mourn for Saul since I have rejected him as king over Israel? Fill your horn with oil and be on your way" (1 Samuel 16:1).

Jesus is the horn of our salvation. Because of Him, we can stop grieving over our past and walking in the shame of our mistakes and failures. We can be on our way about the business of living for the Kingdom. As we get older we don't take as many hits along the way, but things tend to hit harder and hurt more. When those hard hits come, we think, *I don't know if I can keep going.* Receive the prophetic word that came to Samuel: Stop grieving over the past, fill your horn with oil and go.

You and I have God's strength and presence to help us move forward. Let your past faults become your fire. If you stay soft and stay present, God is there. Where you are weak, He will be strong. Not only is He strong for you, but He strengthens you on the inside.

It's in the situations of suffering that I've seen God work to build authority and peace that stay within us well beyond those situations, into the future. Because He loves us, God often puts us through a long process of forming us for Himself. Our resolution must be to press in—press in past the crowds who snicker, shun, accuse, reject and discourage us with hopelessness. When we press in past these, His presence embraces us. He is in His Church. No matter what brokenness or wrong our past has caused, He will use our brokenness to restore us. We just have to dare to risk love again and to forgive, stay soft and remain open to the treasure He's able to bring into any situation.

11 // Doubt Is No Disqualifier

I believe in Christianity as I believe that the sun has risen: not only because I see it, but because by it I see everything else.

—C. S. Lewis

After Jesus' death the eleven disciples were gathered together, and Jesus met them. "When they saw him, they worshiped him—but some of them doubted!" (Matthew 28:17 NLT). Jesus said to them,

> Go into all the world and preach the gospel to all creation. Whoever believes and is baptized will be saved, but whoever does not believe will be condemned. And these signs will accompany those who believe: In my name they will drive out demons; they will speak in new tongues; they will pick up snakes with their hands; and when they drink deadly poison, it will not hurt them at all; they will place their hands on sick people, and they will get well.
>
> Mark 16:15–18

Then as Jesus was blessing them, He was taken up into heaven. In the eleven disciples He left behind, we find eleven reasons to be encouraged. They lived with Jesus. They saw Him walk on water. They were there when He multiplied food, healed the sick and raised the dead. After His resurrection, He spent days with them. He ate with them. They touched the holes in His hands and sides. They worshiped Him as He ascended into heaven by the hand of God.

And some of them doubted?

Jesus didn't even distinguish between those who doubted and those who didn't. He didn't say, "And those of you who doubt, you need to sit down and get your heads screwed on right. Just keep reading the Scriptures and going to synagogue until you get rid of all of that doubt. Then when you have it all figured out, go and make disciples of the nations, healing the sick and driving out demons." He looked at them, and as they were standing there face-to-face with Him, doubting Him, He said,

All authority in heaven and on earth has been given to me. Therefore go and make disciples of all nations, baptizing them in the name of the Father and of the Son and of the Holy Spirit, and teaching them to obey everything I have commanded you. And surely I am with you always, to the very end of the age.

Matthew 28:18–20

The disciples then went out and preached the Kingdom of God. Everywhere they went, God confirmed their work with accompanying signs.

Contending for the Promise

Unbelief and doubt are not the same. Doubt doesn't separate us from the love of God. It doesn't keep us from doing the things

Jesus did. It doesn't keep us from being His disciples. It doesn't disqualify us from His calling. He said "Go" and "I am with you always." As you go, as you do, as you obey, your beliefs will change. Your beliefs follow your actions.

We can live by what our experiences say is true about us, or we can live by what God says is true about us. My dear friend Chris Overstreet, who came to Christ in jail and had never experienced God using him to heal anybody before, took a three-by-five index card and wrote Mark 16:17–20 on it, the verses about those who believed healing the sick. He carried it with him everywhere, reading it throughout the day. He prayed for people and started seeing people healed. Today he is the outreach pastor at Bethel Church and Bethel School of Supernatural Ministry in Redding, California, and he has seen hundreds of people healed. This is a picture of what it means to take hold of the Kingdom of God.

Jesus said, "From the days of John the Baptist until now, the kingdom of heaven has been forcefully advancing, and forceful men lay hold of it" (Matthew 11:12 NIV1984). All throughout Scripture we see that God's heart is *moved* by men and women who take hold of His promises and contend for them. To engage these words of God is to engage in relationship with God. His promises are not the ending of the story; they are the starting place of the adventure He wants to accomplish through us and in us.

Every promise from God is a commissioning. We see this in Moses, Miriam, Abraham, Samuel, Esther, Ruth, David, Gideon, Daniel, Habakkuk, Ezekiel, Anna, Rachel and Mary the mother of Jesus, to name a few. These were men and women who were not perfect by any stretch of the imagination, but who were considered friends of God because of the way they engaged God's promises. This is the legacy of faith we've inherited. God's promises are some of the most intimate things He shares with us. He does not give us His promises so that we'll ignore them. Ignoring His promises is like ignoring His heart.

None of the disciples were qualified to reach the nations. According to people who heard them talk, they probably wouldn't have scored too high on the ACT either. They weren't well educated or people of influence or of much expertise in anything besides fishing. But Jesus said He would be with them always, even till the end of the age. It was a promise they could take hold of.

Don't look to your past to determine your future. Look to what God is calling you to do. Introspection can sometimes be a trap. Satan will try to keep your focus on you and keep your thoughts focused on justifying your unbelief about why you can't do things or how you aren't qualified. You have God with you, though, and as you step out with Him in doing the things He did and reaching out to the people around you, He will equip you.

A big part of being childlike is looking to the future with expectations that are not limited to our past experiences or limited by the world as we currently know it. The world is being undone and remade every day. As we are reborn in God, we need to be renewed in our minds and live in the expectation that things we've never experienced before are possible (see Romans 12:2). Jesus' life is full of promise to us, so "let us run with perseverance the race marked out for us, fixing our eyes on Jesus, the pioneer and perfecter of faith" (Hebrews 12:1–2). As we fix our eyes on Him, the one who is writing His story in us and through us, anything is possible.

Our journey from glory to glory might include a little doubt along the way, but we're to continue with everything God has opened up to us until our lives look exactly like the source—Jesus.

Writing to the Galatians, Paul describes feeling labor pains and groaning continuously "until Christ is fully developed in your lives" (Galatians 4:19 NLT). By definition, maturing in Christ is a process that requires moving beyond where we're at now to a place where we haven't yet arrived. Like Paul, can you feel the squeeze? It's normal to experience doubt because we're called to the unknown. Everything we're destined to be in Christ goes above and beyond anything we've ever been in the past. Look at the disciples—their entire lifestyle of following Jesus involved constant shock and confusion about the things He was telling them to do. We live our lives in that stretch, too.

For some unknown reason, we're looking to feel a sense of security from God's promise in Philippians 1:6 to complete the work He started in us. Really, it's much more like an Olympic swim coach telling you he won't stop until he makes you into the exact likeness of Michael Phelps. Sounds great—until you show up to swim practice the next morning and realize exactly what that means. If you're ever going to break any records, first you're going to do some things you never thought you'd want to do.

Letting Christ live in us means living a lifestyle of constant record breaking. In some ways it's simple; Matthew 11:30 says His yoke is easy and His burden light. He has also given us a new nature. What makes it hard is when we try to drag our old selves along. We try to carry along our past expectations, past history and past failure rate. That causes us to look to ourselves as the determining factor in every situation, instead of looking to God. It leads to striving. The only thing the Bible tells us to strive for is to enter His rest (see Hebrews 4:11). We battle to rest in Him. As we learn to trust that He will live His life through us on a weekly, daily and moment-to-moment basis, however, impossible things start to happen. Going from glory to glory means constantly pushing the limits of anything we did or expected to do in the past.

That's why the Christian life is a life of faith. In the Vineyard, we say that faith is spelled R-I-S-K. If you want to lose weight, you have to go through a little hunger. If you want to do the things Jesus did, you have to go through a little R-I-S-K. It sounds obvious, yet we constantly find ways to sidestep it, and then we wonder why we don't see things change. We avoid risk at all costs, and yet it's the price of the Kingdom. Nobody ever entered the Kingdom of God without it. Going further in and higher up in the Kingdom of God always involves greater and greater risk. The pursuit of God is always a risk. When Moses braved the thundering mountain to encounter God, he risked instant death. When Peter called out to Jesus on the water, it was at tremendous risk. Peter didn't ask Jesus, "Make me walk on water." He got out of the boat and walked toward Jesus, and his pursuit of Christ made the way for a miracle to happen.

Think about when Jesus sent out His 72 followers. They weren't necessarily ready in the sense that we would expect. They were confused and perplexed. Many of them abandoned Jesus a few verses later, when He talked about the blood and body of Christ. Yet He sent them out with simplicity and they returned with joy, saying, "Lord, even the demons submit to us in your name" (Luke 10:17). That wasn't something He had promised them, yet as they went out in obedience, the Kingdom of God broke out all around them.

Healing the sick, casting out demons, multiplying food and raising the dead are all illustrations of the Kingdom message: The King is here! Wherever the King is, we experience King stuff. God's power breaking in is a by-product of His message and His presence in you. As you go, He will show.

Feeding Five Thousand

I love the story of the loaves and fishes. I can just picture what it must have been like. The desert heat beating down amidst the steady drone of cicadas. The feeling of over five thousand hot, sweaty bodies, those who have walked for miles to hear this man speak. Most of these people have been up since before sunrise. They're packed together, straining to hear, straining to catch a glimpse of Him. Occasionally, a little wind picks up dust from the hillside and coats everybody with tiny grains of sand that get stuck in their hair, eyes, every part of their clothing. And there's no food. By late afternoon, the kids are out of control. The older people are starting to feel dizzy, shielding their eyes from the sun and scanning the horizon, waiting for the shadows to grow longer.

You and the other disciples huddle together to form a plan. Now you approach Jesus and present God with your plan to solve your problem. (Shouldn't you be asking Him for His plan instead?) You all tell Him that He needs to send everybody away to buy food.

He replies, "No, *you* feed them!"

Is He being a smart aleck? "We don't have enough," you protest.

"Give Me what you have," He says.

Andrew runs back and hands Jesus five biscuits and two little smoked fish, and then adds, "See, we told You we didn't have enough."

Jesus seems pleased, but you have no idea why. He prays over the bread and fish and then breaks it up and hands you some pieces. He divides it between twelve men, so what you get is probably one small handful. He has the crowds sit down in groups of fifty and then turns to you—nodding at the little bit of bread and fish in your hand. You know this is barely enough to make a dent in your own stomach pains. It's going to be a long, hungry night.

Then He says, "Start feeding that first group of fifty people." *Excuse me?* Ten thousand hungry eyes are fixed on you. You steal a sideways glance at the nearest group. It's a bunch of fishermen from the other shore. You used to go to school with some of them. They were up all night working and then came to hear this talk, and you heard them snickering and cracking jokes at some of the stuff Jesus was saying. Kind of a tough crowd. Your stomach growls, and you can smell the smoky saltiness of the fish in your hand.

Jesus is waiting. "Go on," He says, smiling in the way only He can.

The only, *only* reason you're *even considering* doing what you're about to do is because it's *Jesus* who told you to do it. Still, it's hard to stare down the reality around you. You look down at your handful of food and then back at the hungry men. Slowly, very slowly . . . you walk toward them. You kind of want to walk past and keep going. I mean, how small do you tear the first piece for that first man? Do you give him a pinch? Or do you just give him half and get this over with sooner rather than later? The others are craning their necks toward you to watch this spectacle. Jesus never tells you what will happen as you go out. He just says to go with what you have in your hand.

It's enough.

Isn't that sometimes how we feel when we hear a commandment like "heal the sick" or "love your enemy" or "do the work of an evangelist always"? We think, *Oh God, not me! Not today! I don't have anything like that to give away.* We think, *Why don't You just multiply a big stack of hot dogs in front of me first? Then I'll be more than happy to manage the food line.*

Isn't what we're already doing hard enough? Holding things together, taking care of family, trying to be a nice person and doing a good job at work. We think, *I'm not even sure I'm managing that well, and You're asking me to do something I know I can't do?* But God's promise to us in Matthew 6:33 is that as we seek first His Kingdom, He *will* take care of the rest.

What's in Your Lunch Bag?

A businessman in my area was wrestling through what it meant to hear God's voice and follow the Holy Spirit in his daily life. One day between meetings, he became really hungry but didn't have much cash on him. He decided to make a quick run to McDonald's and pick up a Happy Meal to tide him over. As he was waiting in line, he felt God was nudging him to buy five hamburgers instead. He thought, *That doesn't make sense. It will use up all my money, and what will I do with five hamburgers, anyway? Doesn't God like Happy Meals?*

This businessman was trying to be sensitive to following the Holy Spirit in everyday life, though, so he decided to go ahead and do it. As he walked out of McDonald's feeling sort of foolish, a bag of burgers in hand, he saw a group of homeless teenagers sitting on the curb. He felt as if God said, "Those hamburgers are for them."

He walked over and asked if the teens were hungry. As he started handing out burgers from the bag, four more homeless kids walked up. He kept passing out hamburgers, and then he realized that somehow he had passed out nine hamburgers. He had bought five hamburgers, but he gave out nine. He shook his head and looked in the bottom of the bag. There was still one hamburger left for him.

God increases what we have as we give it away. We're always saying, "Increase it first, and I'll give it." That wasn't how it worked when Jesus fed the five thousand, and that's not how it works with us.

Speaking of what's for lunch, I don't know about you, but lunchtime in the schoolyard was an awkward experience for me. There were always the kids whose moms made them great lunches. They had the cool kind of chips, fancy-looking cookies and juice boxes. My mom was much too practical for that. She packed leftovers in my lunchbox. I'd try to wait until all the other kids were eating, and then slowly, I'd bring out my lunch and try to keep it at least half hidden under my bag. It was usually beans and rice, but sometimes she packed me a sandwich. Middle school kids don't miss much. My childhood friends Pam and Lyndee Guest often would share their lunches with me. They had big hearts that helped ease my isolated feeling in many ways in junior high.

When we think about how God can use us, we may not feel as though we have much to offer. We may feel as if our prayers don't have much faith behind them, and we may feel like the kid with the leftover beans in his lunchbox. But we shouldn't let that stop us. Even doubt has at least a portion of faith mixed in. If we won't do whatever we can, how can God do what we cannot—through us?

What strikes me was that in all of His miracles, Jesus didn't make something from nothing. He made wine from dirty water. He multiplied food from someone's small lunch. He borrowed someone's pet colt. He told Peter to go catch a fish and then take a coin out of its mouth. He even made mud from the dust of the ground to heal a blind man's eyes. However small it may seem, Jesus will use whatever we offer Him. He actually *likes* to use what we have to offer. If we're willing to believe

Him enough to obey, He's willing to help our unbelief (see Mark 9:24).

We still have a problem, though, thinking there are some things we can do and some things we can't do as Christ followers. We have no problem volunteering at soup kitchens, giving away clothes to the needy or sponsoring a child in Africa. We say, "Aw, what a Christian thing to do." Yet *Christian* means "little version of Christ," so actually, throwing out demons, walking on water, multiplying food for thousands, healing the sick and raising the dead should also make us say, "Aw, what a Christian thing to do." *Those* are the things that Jesus did.

Sometimes we also stop ourselves by saying, "I just don't know if this is the will of God—Jesus only did what He saw the Father doing." Yes, Jesus did what He saw the Father doing, and look at His life! If we just do what Jesus did, we'll be doing the will of the Father, too. We don't stop and wonder, *Does God want me to give this bowl of soup to this poor child?* We already know. In the same way, we can have the same confidence and joy in releasing healing over the sick and encouraging people who are far from God that salvation is here.

Raised from a Coma

I was at a Vineyard national conference in Costa Rica, and a man from the church called us to go to the hospital to pray for his brother. Amoebas had entered his ear and were eating into his brain. We prayed with him in the ICU, and nothing seemed to change. Feeling kind of defeated, I headed out the door with my hosts. As we were walking out, I noticed a woman who I felt might have lower back and hip problems. I asked her if she struggled with pain in these areas, and she said yes.

I said, "If you'll let me pray for you, God will heal you right now." I prayed for her and then asked what her pain level was. "Zero!" she said. God had completely healed her in that moment, through one prayer. Then she said, "Wait!" and went running into one of the back rooms down the hall. She returned breathless and asked, "Would you please come pray for my father-in-law? He's been in a coma for many months."

Even though I'd been discouraged, I decided to go for it. I said, "Absolutely, if you promise me you'll go to the nurses' station and get them all to come in."

She went and convinced a doctor and several nurses to come into the room. Typically, few people are more disbelieving of what I'm doing than people who work around sickness and death every day. In front of this medical staff, I prayed, "Father, I thank You for Your miraculous, mighty power. Thank You that You're going to heal this man right now and raise him up from a coma so that everyone will know that You're here and in pursuit of a relationship with them."

Then I addressed the man in the coma: "Pablo—wake up right now in the name of Jesus!"

Pablo's eyes popped open. It actually scared me, but it was also one of the coolest things I've seen.

His daughter-in-law screamed and ran out of the room to get his wife. Three of the nurses also shrieked and ran out. The doctor started checking Pablo. He was fully awake and responsive. Within five minutes, people from all of the other rooms started calling for us to come and pray for them. Faith spread like wildfire, from nothing.

We never know what God is going to do or where we'll see breakthrough happen when we least expect it. As His children, we just walk in confidence that where we are, God is. Our job is to step out and expect God's best to step in.

Recognize and Resist the Lies

As we step out and go for it, we need to stay sharp so that we can recognize and resist the lies of the enemy. The devil is always trying to get us to doubt what we already have, to second-guess ourselves, to stammer and to hold back. Satan has come against God's people since the Garden, challenging them that they could be "like" God, when in reality they already were like God—made in His image and given dominion over the earth.

Satan almost always tempts us with something that we already have in God. God had just publicly affirmed Jesus by saying, "You are My beloved Son; in You I am well pleased" (Luke 3:22 NKJV). Almost immediately, Satan countered with his first temptation of Jesus: "*If* You are the Son of God, command this stone to become bread" (Luke 4:3 NKJV, emphasis added). Just as he did with Jesus, Satan first tries to talk us out of what God has already said is true about us. His goal is to convince us that we can't do what God has told us to do. How did Jesus know He was the Son of God? I believe He knew it through faith, the same way we do. As a human, He had never been to heaven. He related to God the same way we do—by spending time alone with Him and being built up in His presence.

Remember that Satan will accuse us with what we can't accomplish and focus all of our attention on our weaknesses and failures. Every single day, however, we have to put off the old self and put on the new self, the new creation that Scripture says we are (see 2 Corinthians 5:17).

The second lie Satan feeds us involves questioning God's Word and His nature. In Genesis 3:1, Satan asked, "Did God really say . . . ?" Satan's challenge was that God was holding back on His children. The question he was asking boiled down to, "Is God good? Does He really have your best interests in mind?" When Satan can get us to question the character of God, everything else unravels. That's what unbelief is.

Truth activates faith; lies destroy faith. When we speak truth to Satan's lies, we destroy them. That's why the Word of God is called a sword. Even as we step out in doing the things we're called to do, we're clearing the way for our faith to grow.

Don't worry about whether or not you have enough faith. If you're able to step out in obedience to see something done, you have enough faith to accomplish it. Other factors may prevent the full results from showing up immediately, but the faith is there simply in taking the risk of stepping out. People aren't great in the Kingdom because they have great willpower or are full of unusual goodness. People are great in the Kingdom because they're learning to put their faith in Christ instead of in themselves.

Do you ever get discouraged? You're not alone. David was the greatest of God's warriors, but he battled discouragement and depression throughout the psalms. David also shows us that in God, we always find a reason to hope—in His power, in His faithfulness, in His mercy and steadfast love. His character is the platform from which we can rejoice our way back to joy.

When we feel down, isn't it because we're putting our hope in ourselves? Throughout Scripture, God tells His valiant men and women, "Do not be afraid; do not be discouraged—*take courage.*" Everything changes when we realize that discouragement is not a state that we must endure, like sadness or suffering. Many times Satan will fight us with the greatest discouragements just before God fulfills our expectation. David's huge calamity of dealing with Jonathan's death came just days before he was finally established as king of Israel. In every situation we face, "we shall reap, if we faint not" (Galatians 6:9 KJV).

Raise Your Expectations

One thing I often encounter as people hear my stories is that they're encouraged and excited to hear the amazing things God has done, but they don't expect that God can use them in the same way. We believe that God can do these things in theory or in someone else, but not in us.

We read Scriptures and think, *Jesus is God; that's why He did these things.* But Jesus left behind His supernatural powers and became fully human, receiving the Holy Spirit the same way we do and becoming an example to us all of what a life of obedience to the Father looks like. He also sent out His disciples to do the things they saw Him do, and then He commissioned all of us and said that we would "do even greater things than these" (John 14:12).

All around the world, we hear incredible testimonies of God's power and miraculous breakthrough—someone just has to go first. When David slew Goliath, he was the first average person to take on a giant. Immediately following that, the Bible records that six more giants were killed by David's men and even by his younger nephew.

Who's willing to go first?

Twin Healings

Several years ago, a man visited our church because he had heard that we pray for people with cancer and see them healed. He had been diagnosed with prostate cancer, and after the service we prayed for him and his wife, who was from the Philippines. Neither of them were churchgoers.

After we prayed for him, I turned to her. "Do you get migraine headaches a lot?" I asked.

"Yes," she said, "I have one right now. My whole life, I've had them. The doctor recently upped my prescription, and it's not getting any better. They can't give me any more medicine or my organs will start shutting down."

I told her, "If you'll let me pray for you, God will heal it right now." Her husband and I prayed for her, and the migraine left immediately and never returned. Later that week, she was telling her twin sister what had happened. Her twin sister lives in Hawaii, and she realized that at the exact same time as her sister was being prayed for in Chicago for a migraine, she had been suffering with a terrible migraine that had suddenly left. Both of them were healed!

Her husband had more testing done after we prayed for him, and no trace of cancer was left in his body. Both he and his wife got on fire for God, and they started coming to our church and attending our Alpha program for new believers. Four weeks into the Alpha course, they approached me. The woman said, "Robby, my mom and my aunt are in the hospital with cancer, and they're dying. We've prayed about it, and we feel as though we're supposed to send you to the Philippines. We'll buy your tickets and send you there to pray for them. Will you go?"

I looked at this couple and answered, "No." The woman looked surprised and a little hurt, but I explained, "If you believe *I* can go and do it, *you* can go and do it."

"Really?" the woman said. She seemed surprised.

"Yes!" I encouraged her. "Don't go small—go big. Do it as publicly as possible. Get the word out in the whole village that your mother and aunt are going to be healed of cancer."

This woman went back to the Philippines and went straight from the airport to the hospital, where she prayed for her aunt and her mom. Both of them were instantly healed. She went back the next day and both ladies were released from the hospital—cancer free. People from the village started coming to the house to see what had happened because they thought that they'd been saying good-bye to these ladies for the last time. The woman started going through our sermon handouts with them, and she would read those aloud and go through the main points with people. She had only been to six or seven church services in her life up to that point, but she was teaching her perspective and telling anecdotal stories. People started coming daily and gathering around the porch to hear her, and they were giving their lives to Christ even though this was in a Muslim area of the Philippines.

Take It to the Streets

John Wimber often said, "The meat is in the street." If we want to see the power back in the Church, we've got to take it to the streets. Jesus came to seek and to save what was lost. He didn't come to establish perfect little enclaves of healed, shiny, happy people. He said "Go." As we go, as we do, as we obey, that's where the real miracle takes place. We're being transformed to be like Him, and we're being stretched and matured through perseverance and the testing of our faith. John chapter 1 says,

> He came to his own, and his own people did not receive him. But to all who did receive him, who believed in his name, he gave the right to become children of God, who were born, not of blood nor of the will of the flesh nor of the will of man, but of God. . . . For from his fullness we have all received, grace upon grace.
>
> verses 11–13, 16 ESV

Our bodies and sicknesses are just temporary. As we follow Jesus, the transformation that takes place within us is eternal, and our job is to bring as many people as possible with us. The fullness of the Kingdom is still to come, but there's a level of the Kingdom that we aren't exercising now because we're not *going*. Do you know where the hope for your city is? It's sitting in your chair right now. God's plan of revival for your city is you—Him working in you and through you. There's no need to wait for something else to come. You've come. And because you've come, Christ has shown up. I pray that you believe that. I pray that you grab hold of God's promises for you. Christ came to seek and to save what was lost and to destroy the works of the enemy. Because taking His power and presence to the streets is important to Him, it's got to be important to you and me.

12 // Raising the Dead

> Perseverance is more than endurance. It is endurance
> combined with absolute assurance and certainty that
> what we are looking for is going to happen. . . . If our
> hopes seem to be experiencing disappointment right
> now, it simply means that they are being purified.
>
> —Oswald Chambers

My son Judah and I are on a mission. It's a mission that has grown up and formed a bond between us as we've faced some pretty hairy situations together. It has come out of circumstances that you could describe as unusual, awkward and even downright disturbing. It's not the typical father-son activity I'd recommend to most. Our mission is to raise the dead. We figure, go big or go home.

We've prayed for several dozen dead people so far; not a lot yet. As this goes to print, we've yet to see anyone come back to life as a result of our prayers. But I haven't had any complaints from the dead people, either.

The Kingdom of God is continuously referred to as a treasure that people give everything to attain. There's no such thing as giving too much. I don't believe any of us will get to heaven and hear God say, "You did a lot of great things, My faithful servant, but I have to tell you, you really spent too much time praying for sick people. You told way too many people about Jesus when you knew they'd probably never understand anyway—you pushed it too far. You asked for too much. It was as if you were honestly trying to give away half of heaven. Save some for the rest of us! And I really need to ask, why did you have to go and pray for those dead people?"

There's way too much out there that we haven't even started to approach yet. Nobody's going to get it all right, but if we're only trying to do what we "know" we can do, we're already setting ourselves up to fall short. We're called to walk in the same sonship that Jesus did, and we're called to persevere. Just like the first disciples, we're in the process of coming into the fullness of the revelation of who Christ is for us. Sometimes the disciples believed; other times they were full of doubt. But God is in the impossible. As the disciples continued to follow Christ and stepped out in doing the things He did, they were strengthened. As they went out to do what they knew they couldn't do, they came into the Kingdom of heaven.

It's a stretch—it always is. Too often, we let fear of failure lock us up. In the parable of the talents, it was fear of failure that caused one of the servants to bury his potential (see Matthew 25:14–30; Luke 19:12–28). To win big, we've got to risk big. If we're not "failing" in what we do on a regular basis, I have a hard time believing we're really going after it. What I want to give away more than anything else in this chapter is the permission to fail, and fail big.

An Unusual After-School Activity

Ring, ring! It was late afternoon, and the phone had been ringing off the hook all day. I looked down at the number. It was my oldest son, Judah, a junior in high school. I picked up the phone and could hear his excitement leaping through the receiver. "Dad! Dad! You *have* to come right now! You *have* to—just say you will! Come right now!"

This was Judah in full throttle, and I knew he wouldn't take no for an answer easily.

"What's going on?" I asked.

"Dad, my friend just got home from school, and her grandmother died. She called me, and she was so sad. Dad, we have to go pray for her grandma to be raised from the dead right now! They don't have anyone else to call. I told her my dad's a minister and we would come pray, and she said yeah, she wants us to do that. Dad, if we can get there *right now*, we can raise her grandma up before the funeral people come!"

The timing couldn't have been worse for me. I told him, "Judah, I really can't. I have a couple of meetings this afternoon with our staff."

"Daaaad!" Judah prevailed. "We have a real dead person here! We have to pray for her. How often do we get to do that? You have to come over!"

He was appealing to the Dawkins logic. Somehow my son has a way with me, and half an hour later we were headed out together. Judah was pumped.

"This is sooo awesome!" he said. "My whole school is going to come to Jesus because we're going to raise the dead!"

We had a shy, very sweet Russian intern named Zhanna living with us at the time. She looked back and forth between Judah and me, and then posed a question tentatively: "I would like to go raise the dead. Can I come, too?"

"Sure," I said, "let's go."

We got to the family's door, and she and Judah were way too excited to be there. I said, "Okay, you both have to be quiet and calm down. A family member has died here; this is an extremely hard time for the family. This is not about us being excited to raise the dead."

Zhanna looked down. "I'm sorry. . . ."

"No, not you!" I told her, shooting my son the stink-eye. Black Bible in hand, we respectfully entered the house. Judah's friend took us back to the room where her grandmother was. The woman's family was gathered around, and I read Psalm 23 out loud. I'd never found myself in this position before and I decided that praying resurrection over the woman might disturb the family, so I asked if we could have a few minutes alone with the grandmother.

They nodded. "Is this to perform the last rites?" one asked.

"Umm . . . sort of," I answered.

As soon as they left the room, I told Judah and Zhanna, "Okay, guys, let's not be too loud; we don't want to disturb them." Then I put my hand under the woman's head and commanded, "Resurrection power, in the name of Jesus, *riiiise*."

Nothing happened. Judah was praying like crazy over her feet, and I said, "Breath of Life, fill these lungs." I blew over her chest. Her hair flew around, but that was it.

After about ten minutes, Judah looked up at me. "Dad, I know what's wrong! Didn't a few people in the Bible lie on top of the dead person?"

I looked at the elderly woman laid out in front of me and said, "Well, a sixteen-year-old boy could get away with it better than a man who is fortyish."

Judah looked at our Russian intern and said, "A Russian girl could get away with it even better; we'll tell them that's what they do in her country."

Zhanna blurted out, "I'm scared now!"

About that time the door opened, and a young man came in with a middle-aged woman walking beside him. The guy said, "All of this stops now!" I looked over and saw the woman's head was cocked to the side. So I blocked her with my body, straightened her head and smoothed her hair back into place.

Almost at the same time, the woman said, "Oh, my gosh, look at Mom! It looks as if her color is coming back; it looks as if she could speak at any moment."

I was like, "Really?"

But the young man spoke over her words, saying, "He's not a priest!" Then he looked at us and said, "You guys aren't Catholic, are you? I'm going to have to ask you to leave."

As soon as he said that, we felt as though the faith was sucked right out of the air. Telling them how sorry we were for their loss, we left the house.

Judah gave his friend a hug as we left. Out on the sidewalk, he showed his disappointment. "Man!" he said, giving me the inch sign with his fingers. "We were that close!"

We drove back to our house in silence. I kept looking over at Judah, who leaned his head up against the car window and stared out in deep thought, his brows furrowed pensively. My heart sank. My boy was discouraged.

"Hey, it's okay," I told my son. "Don't feel too bad about it. We did the best we could."

"What do you mean?" he asked in surprise.

"Are you feeling discouraged?" I prompted.

"Oh, no way, Dad!" he told me brightly. "I'm not thinking about that. I'm just thinking about the next time we pray for someone to rise from the dead and how it's going to happen. I'm just trying to think of how we can get hold of more dead people. That's the ticket, Dad. We gotta pray for more dead people!" I wiped a tear from my eye in pride.

Pushing to Failure

Push to failure is a term used in weight lifting and body building. It's when you push to the absolute end of your strength and the weight drops because you can't push it any longer. You will hear trainers at the gym shout, "Push to failure! Failure is the goal!" When you hit failure, the most muscle growth occurs.

We avoid failure, but pushing the limits to failure is when we learn the most about risk and learn how far we can go. When I was in middle school, I had a teacher who never gave anyone a 100 percent score on her tests. I told her she was the worst teacher because of it. She turned to me and said, "Robby, if you got 100 percent on a test, it probably means you aren't learning anything. When you miss something, I see what I need to teach you." I then conceded that if that was the goal, then she was the best teacher.

When we delight ourselves in obedience, we don't get discouraged in the process. Our idea of success is the perfect healing, the clear prophetic word, the complete deliverance. The disciples rejoiced at seeing signs and wonders, but Jesus corrected them, saying no, instead, "Rejoice that your names are written in heaven" (Luke 10:20). Jesus says it's more about our identity than the miraculous. God's idea of success is our obedience. The results are for Him, not us.

God is after our obedience. When we're "pushing to failure," it helps take our focus off the results as our measure of success.

If our ministry is based on "results," there's a danger that the ministry can become about us. When the disciples went out doing the things that Jesus did, the results were most often riots, stoning, beating and incarceration. That's not exactly your seeker-sensitive approach to ministry. From cover to cover, the Bible shows God calling men and women into the impossible. It's in the impossible that God reveals Himself and calls us forth into what we are meant to be. He calls all His people to dream big and to believe Him. What are you asking God for? How big are your prayers?

Paul did a great job contextualizing the Gospel message for the Greeks. He appealed to their love of knowledge, their understanding of spiritual matters and their lifestyle of discourse and debate (see Acts 17). His message was popular at first—he could have stopped sooner and been the most popular speaker of the day. But then he came to the cross and the power of Christ's resurrection message. At the point, some turned away in disgust, others thought they'd like to hear him again, and others believed and were saved. Everywhere he went Paul met with success, but he also met with many who were ready to kill him. That's pushing to failure.

Fear of failure locks us up, as does fear of people. God's promise to Jeremiah was fulfilled centuries ago, and it still stands today: "Go wherever I send you and say whatever I tell you. And don't be afraid of the people, for I will be with you and will protect you. I, the Lord, have spoken!" (Jeremiah 1:7–8 NLT). Yet the very thing Jeremiah experienced back in Old Testament times is still one of the main things that prevents us now from fulfilling our mission in God. Fear of people can keep us from telling anybody about Jesus.

When we see failure as part of our goal, however, we are free to walk in the footsteps of Jesus. Jesus came and lived and died for His people. He was betrayed and handed over, then slain by the leaders of the very people for whom He gave everything. That's failure. That's the failure we face every day when we worry, *What if they think I'm weird? What if they think I'm wasting their time? What if they get mad? What if they hate me and think I'm stupid?*

If that's the worst that can happen, it's not that bad. God provides for our needs in every situation. We have to realize that God our Father is willing to provide for us. As long as I'm doing His will, He provides for it. In every area of gifting, if we steward rightly, He will provide. Pursue the way of love and don't be afraid to just go for it. Who knows? You might change someone's life forever. Something you say, an act of kindness, a healing, a prayer or just the bold faith you show in stepping out to obey God could make all the difference in someone's life.

There's no risk-free way to do this and still see stuff happen. If you're going to go for it, just go big. Don't shrink back. It helps to remember that none of us can heal anybody. Only God can do that. In my personal paraphrase of Mark 16's Great Commission, God says, "You go, and I'll show."

Death in the Park

I was invited to teach at my friend Rey Matos's church in Puerto Rico. I greatly admire this friend, a brilliant scientist and author whose church does tremendous social justice work all over Latin America. At his church conference, I asked the guys to please let me know if anyone died during the weekend because I wanted to raise them from the dead.

Rey's eyebrows shot up questioningly when he heard that, and he asked me later what I had in mind. The next day I got a chance to show him. A young man came running in to us and said, "Pastor, Pastor, I was two blocks down and a guy dropped dead in the park."

I looked at Rey. "Come on with me!" I practically dragged him to the scene in the park. It was slightly intimidating. The ambulance had arrived. They had the man hooked up to a monitor, and the screen was completely flatlined. The paramedics were examining the guy and filling out paperwork.

I asked the men, "Excuse me, we're ministers. Can we pray for this man?"

They looked at each other and back at me. "He's dead."

"Yes, we know. We want to pray for him to rise from the dead."

After some back-and-forth, they shook their heads yes, that we could, but only until the police arrived. At that point, I practically jumped on the dead guy. A policeman friend of mine who has prayed and seen some people rise from the dead told me once that there's something about chest-to-chest contact that's like imparting life. There's also biblical precedent for full-body contact, so I decided whatever I had, I was going to try to give it away as fast as I could. I bent over him so I was chest-to-chest and started commanding him authoritatively, "Rise up! Rise up in the name of Jesus!"

I was commanding life in the park, and for some reason a crowd started to gather around the scene. At one point I put my hand on his chest, and I blew on him and said, "I impart to you the Breath of Life."

Suddenly I saw his cheeks start quivering, as if he wanted to speak. I looked at Rey wide-eyed, but Rey just shook his head back at me.

"I think you're pushing too hard on his stomach," Rey said.

I took my hand off the guy's belly, and sure enough his cheeks sank back to the same lifeless expression. Around that time, the police showed up. They quickly worked to clear everyone away from the scene. It was then that I realized that many of the people who were standing there watching had tears in their eyes. I asked Rey if they had known the man.

"No," he said, "they're saying, 'Look at the courage. Look at the faith. Look at these men who actually believe their God.'"

I noticed people still watching us as we left, and I turned and invited them to church: "If any of you know somebody who needs healing, come this weekend to the church."

That Sunday, twelve different people from that scene in the park came up to us at church, and two of them gave their lives to Christ. Those people were all affected because of a complete and total failure. Two of them had their lives forever changed—out of pushing to failure. When it seems as if nothing's working, we have no idea how God is at work.

Willing to Fail—and Fail Big

If I could go back again, knowing the people I prayed for wouldn't be raised from the dead, I'd absolutely pray over them again in the same way. We don't know what's happening behind the scenes until we get to heaven. Every time we pray, something is happening, whether we can observe it immediately or not. Romans 14:23 defines sin as anything that does not proceed from faith: "Everything that does not come from faith is sin." I believe in the same way, every act of faith has a powerful expression in the spiritual realm that is breaking down the power of darkness in this world. Church history records that hundreds would come to faith through the death of a martyr. Tertullian, called the father of Western Christianity, wrote, "The blood of the martyrs is the seed of the church." The martyrs' deaths were acts of faith that shattered the strongholds of powers and principalities in the kingdom of darkness.

Martyrdom might be the ultimate expression of faith, but isn't it also the ultimate failure? The ultimate risk? Those who gave their lives knew they would never see any of the results of their faith, yet their final perseverance launched the movement that has transformed the face of the world. The martyrs were willing to die for God and call Him good, without being offended at death. Even in death, so much of their testimony was trusting that a God who became a man to die for them had not abandoned them, regardless of the situation. Faith is simply one step of certainty against the onslaught of uncertainty. The question isn't, are we willing to die for Christ? The question is, are we willing to live a life of risk for Him? Being willing to fail and fail big in the arena of living out a lifestyle of risky evangelism frees us from fear and sets us up to do the impossible. Are we willing to look foolish for Jesus?

What if failure is actually the goal? Too often, we hit failure and quit. The level we're at now is where we succeed. Where we fail is the level we're going to next. What if we keep praying for person after person—asking for healing, listening in prayer, sharing the Gospel—and absolutely nothing happens? From what I've seen myself and heard from others, that probably won't happen. If it does, let me encourage you that failure is actually the goal. We have to keep our expectations high. If you're having trouble and getting discouraged while praying for sick people, try praying for a dead person. Push a boulder until you're strong enough to throw stones. The battles we win in private and in the backstreets determine the success of the battles we win in public when everyone's watching.

We have limits, but let's make sure the holdup isn't on our end. You have to decide what you really want and go after it. When you're clear about where you're headed, it's so much easier for those daily life decisions to fall in line. No matter what your goal is, many days of persevering in the mundane choices lie ahead in order to reach it. It's the law of the farm—what you sow bountifully, you reap bountifully. Give it all you've got, and when you reach your capacity, ask God to expand your capacity.

So often we accommodate casual Christianity and then wonder why there's not more power in our lives. God desires that we have more power, but we short-circuit it. We hold high ideals but see few results because we have an aversion to risk, and we develop our lifestyle around this aversion. We prefer to think of Christianity as a religious philosophy rather than as a top-down revolution meant to turn the powers of darkness on their heads. We're in a culture that trains us to live by feelings, emotions and our desires instead of living with real clarity. The presence of God is countercultural to the norms of discouragement, depression and fear that most people live with. As we press in to God, He renews our vision, our sense of freedom and our expectations. We experience joy that's almost illogical and passion that fuels our resilience in all circumstances. Keep expecting big from heaven, and keep persevering in the grit of daily life. You'd be surprised how often the two coincide.

Almost . . .

Around 10 p.m. one night, I got a call from the police department. "Robby, would you be willing to come down to the hospital? A man has died, and his son is asking for a minister. We suspect foul play, so we want a police chaplain on the scene."

As a chaplain for the Aurora police department, I'd been trained in how to handle situations that involved a potential crime scene. The man had suddenly gone unconcious the day before, had fallen into a coma and was put on life support. His wife had come to the hospital that evening and requested that he be taken off life support. He had been dead about two hours when I arrived at the scene. His son had been there and had called for a chaplain.

As soon as the police called me, I left my house and met the family at the hospital. The dead man's wife was in the waiting room and eyed me as I came in. She seemed frightened and was crying. I was wearing my police jacket, so she pointed me down the hall to the room where the body was. The man's son was in the room, still weeping. He was nineteen or twenty years old. A nurse was taking some of the equipment away from the body.

I asked the young man, "Did you request a chaplain?"

He nodded.

I told him, "I'm really sorry for your loss."

He nodded and looked over to his dad.

I told him, "This may sound crazy, but we could pray for him to be raised from the dead. God still raises people from the dead."

His son looked down and asked, "I know Jesus was raised from the dead and people in the Bible, too, but does that still happen now?"

I told him, "I've had friends who prayed and saw dead people restored, and I've seen videos and testimonies. But it's fully up to you. I can't guarantee it will happen, but I believe and I know that God does this today, and I would love to pray with you for your father, if you want me to."

The son agreed.

The nurse came back through the room and asked, "Are you guys praying for him?"

"Actually, we're praying for him to rise from the dead," I said.

The nurse raised an eyebrow and said, "I gotta see this!"

There are things I know now about praying for the dead that I didn't know then, but as I was praying for the man, immediately I could feel God's presence in the room. The son started feeling the power of God, too, and he started having difficulty standing up.

"What's happening?" he asked me.

The nurse added, "I'm feeling a little dizzy myself."

I told them, "You may need to sit down. That's God's presence, God's power."

The man's head suddenly jerked to one side, as if he were dodging a fly.

His son asked, "Did you see that?"

"Yes," I said carefully. I didn't want to get him too excited.

All of a sudden the father's fingers began twitching. A finger would stretch out in a sudden twitch, and then another one would, and then the same one would twitch again. Sometimes nerves can twitch after death, but not repeatedly in that way.

When that started happening, the nurse jumped up and said, "I gotta get out of here!" and ran out of the room.

On the other side, the man's elbow also twitched slightly. When I had first come into the room, he was clearly dead. His eyes seemed almost as if they were sealed closed, and he had a waxy look to him. Now his eyes seemed shut only slightly, and a couple of times it seemed as if he blinked with his eyes closed. There were also several slight flinches. I started getting more and more engaged.

The son said, "Do you think he's coming back?"

I replied, "It looks like it to me."

About five minutes had passed since the nurse had run out, and then the head nurse came in and said we had to stop praying.

"Can we spend a few more minutes in here?" I asked.

"No!" the nurse said. "This has to stop! The spouse doesn't want you to keep going."

We hadn't told anyone else what we were doing, but it was clear that the nurse must have told the mother and the other nurses what was happening.

I told the son, "You can decide to keep praying if you want to." The head nurse was firm. "No, he can't! The wife is the closest family member listed. She makes the decision."

I was representing the police department, so I had to leave at the wife's request. I thanked the son and excused myself. The police never made any case surrounding the man; the only thing I heard was that he was cremated the next morning. This was another experience where I believe I saw the power of God present for resurrection. Though I didn't see it happen that time, I'm going to keep pressing in to praying for the dead to rise.

Plundering the Enemy

We get so caught up in wondering what God's will is, but we've already been given a pretty tall order in Scripture—God *wills* for His Son, Jesus, to live out His life through us. He's given us the Holy Spirit, He's given us power and He's given us authority to carry on in Christ's ministry of reconciliation, proclaiming and demonstrating the Kingdom of God and destroying the works of Satan. It's open season, and every one of us was licensed when we received the Holy Spirit. When demons saw Jesus, they screamed out, "What have we to do with You, Jesus of Nazareth? Did You come to destroy us?" because they knew exactly what His presence meant—the kingdom of darkness had to go (Luke 4:34 NKJV). Christ came to destroy the power of death and set us free from its fear. Hebrews 2:14–15 (ESV) describes it this way:

> Since therefore the children share in flesh and blood, he himself likewise partook of the same things, that through death he might destroy the one who has the power of death, that is, the devil, and deliver all those who through fear of death were subject to lifelong slavery.

Christ's life and death on the cross "bound the strong man," and He commissioned His disciples in the ministry of plundering the strong man's house and dividing the spoils (see Mark 3:27; Luke 11:22). Throughout His teaching, Jesus compares God's Kingdom and its fruits to treasure, to the harvest, to plundered goods and to pearls to be sought after. Pursuing these things is not just for the spiritually elite; it's for everyone. In that same statement He made about plundering the strong man's house, Jesus said, "Whoever is not with me is against me, and whoever does not gather with me scatters" (Luke 11:23 ESV). We can gather with freedom and joy, and without ever fearing that seeking the Kingdom of God in every circumstance might be "outside the will of God" for us.

Turn Up the Impudence?

In Scripture, we never see Jesus turning away a request for healing or a request to raise the dead. In fact, He rebukes the people around Him for not asking for more of the things of the Spirit. In Luke 11:5–13, Jesus describes for His disciples an impudent neighbor who makes some late-night demands on his friend, a tall order after midnight. He urges His followers to show that same persistence: "Ask, and it will be given to you; seek, and you will find; knock, and it will be opened to you. For everyone who asks receives, and the one who seeks finds, and to the one who knocks it will be opened" (Luke 11:9–10 ESV).

Jesus basically tells His disciples that we humans have a limited, corrupted understanding of God's goodness, one that He far and above surpasses. We don't have to fear pursuing the Kingdom too hard. It's our inheritance; it's what we were made for. Some people pray for the safety of their families and kids. I pray, "Lord, make my boys the most *dangerous* men on the planet."

When Elijah confronted the prophets of Baal on Mount Carmel, he didn't shrink back. He turned up the risk level. Israel had turned to the worship of Baal, the priests and prophets of God had been murdered and the land had been in drought for three years. The word of God came to Elijah, "Go and present yourself to Ahab, and I will send rain on the land" (1 Kings 18:1).

It was a word of mercy, but it was also a word of risk. Ahab was Elijah's sworn enemy who for three years had searched the land to kill him. Throughout Scripture, God uses people's actions and responses of faith to release His promises. The thirsty land cried out for water, but Elijah knew that even more than rain, restoration was needed. He presented himself to Ahab and sent to gather the leaders, the people and the prophets of Baal upon Mount Carmel. He challenged the prophets of Baal to prepare a sacrifice and call for their god to send down fire to consume the sacrifice. All day long, four hundred prophets of Baal prayed and cried and danced and cut themselves with swords, as was their custom. There was no response, no one answered, no one paid attention. The day drew to a close.

Elijah then called the people over and prepared the altar of God. He rebuilt it with twelve stones representing the identity of God's people. It also served as a reminder to both God and

Israel of God's covenant with Jacob, "to whom the word of the LORD had come, saying, 'Your name shall be Israel'" (verse 31).

Not only did Elijah build an altar; he also surrounded it with a moat. Notice that God didn't tell him to dig the trench or pour in the water. This was Elijah turning up the risk. In a time of drought, he poured out a compelling sacrifice—three years of no rain, and three times he poured out a sacrifice of four large jars of water. Twelve jugs of water poured out over twelve stones was probably more water than most of the people had seen in three years. Was this the last of the supply, dragged up the mountainside for a people who had been standing all day in the desert sun?

Elijah poured the water down the sides of the altar, filling the moat. It was a sacrifice that cried out to God, "We need You more than water!"

Burning the Boats

Commanders in ancient times often ordered their soldiers to burn the boats upon landing on enemy territory. It was an all-out commitment to the cause—to return as heroes in conquered ships, with no alternative. For Elijah, pouring out this quantity of water in a time of drought was essentially burning the boats—refusing to hoard any provision other than that which God had promised. Trusting that God would provide, Elijah put everything on the line, stretching himself out before God and before Israel. He didn't hold back. He prayed, "Answer me, LORD, answer me, so these people will know that you, LORD, are God, and that you are turning their hearts back again" (verse 37). After he prayed, "the fire of the LORD fell and burned up the sacrifice, the wood, the stones and the soil, and also licked up the water in the trench" (verse 38). Notice God wasn't offended by Elijah's expectancy and risk taking.

Elijah moved and spoke in faith. Though there wasn't a cloud in the sky, he told Ahab, "Go, eat and drink, for there is the sound of a heavy rain" (verse 41). There wasn't even moisture in the air, yet Elijah didn't shrink back. He climbed to the top of Carmel, bent down to the ground, put his face between his knees and seven times sent his servant to scan the horizon for rain. Finally, when there was just a tiny cloud the size of a man's fist rising in the distance from the sea, Elijah had his servant warn Ahab, "Hitch up your chariot and go down before the rain stops you" (verse 44).

God had said He was sending rain, and without a cloud on the horizon Elijah had summoned the king and had performed the ultimate showdown. He didn't hold back; he pushed to failure. We need to push to failure, too, because the kingdom of darkness is like a drought whose expiration date has passed. Jesus came proclaiming "the year of the Lord's favor" and that "the Kingdom of God is at hand," and then He sent us out to the nations to proclaim God's favor and grace to all peoples. Seeing the Kingdom at work is a privilege that ancient eyes longed to see.

The Kingdom of heaven is at hand—now present in believers, and once and for all present with the return of the King. We've been commissioned to prepare the way, and as far as I'm concerned, that means everything is fair game—even raising the dead. We're not waiting around to be sent; we've already been sent. Sometimes God may stop us from going a certain direction. We see this with some of His followers in Acts 16:6 when the Holy Spirit checked them from preaching in the province of Asia. God didn't chastise them for going, He just redirected their mission.

I once was determined to go into full-time overseas missions, but God checked me each time from relocating my family overseas. Now I've been able to go out and take them with me, traveling and ministering overseas in nations I'd never even dreamed of. The understanding is that we're all operating on a "Go." As long as our desire and willingness are there, God will direct us—and sometimes redirect us. In the process, He will open doors for us that we never thought possible.

13 // Perseverance

Don't Let Discouragement Win

Wherever there is a Church obeying the words and doing the works of Jesus, there is an outpost of the Kingdom of God. And the outpost is always in the middle of hostile territory. . . .

—John Wimber

God can use a failure. The Bible is full of them. What God can't use is a quitter.

—Pastor Bob Dawkins[1]

God tells us to go, and He doesn't airbrush the photo too much. His tagline probably could have used a little work from the marketing department, though. He says, "I am sending you out like lambs among wolves" (Luke 10:3). That encouraging picture didn't make the brochure, did it? We're sent out as lambs among wolves, led by the "Lamb standing, as though it had been slain" (Revelation 5:6 ESV).

We saw in the previous chapter that Elijah was a lamb standing among four hundred wolves. We're told, "Elijah was a man with a nature like ours, and he prayed fervently that it might not rain, and for three years and six months it did not rain on the earth" (James 5:17 ESV). He had mountaintop highs, yet he also battled fear and discouragement. Directly after his mountaintop showdown of all time with Baal's prophets, he received a death threat from Queen Jezebel. He was afraid and ran for his life into the wilderness, where he prayed that he might die. He was so desperate and felt so much loneliness and pain that he cried, "I have had enough, LORD. . . . Take my life; I am no better than my ancestors" (1 Kings 19:4). Then he curled up under a bush and fell asleep.

Pastoring in a poor urban setting, I've often found myself teetering in this place of tremendous victory and tremendous discouragement. It's difficult and yet very rewarding. When we first moved to Aurora, the chief of police at the time, David Stover, told me, "Ministering here in Aurora will bring your greatest agony and hopefully some victory."

I wasn't much encouraged by those words, but I've since found them to be true. There's the financial stress, the pressure and weight of the ministry, the people whom you help or work with that turn around and hate you. You help turn their lives around, and then they're upset with you. Sometimes it has been a fight just to stay in it.

The death of Johnny Beiler was one huge blow that caught me broadside and was hard to overcome. That Johnny had come to our church was nothing short of a miracle. He had been standing on a ladder with a noose around his neck, about to take the final jump to end his life, when his phone rang. It was a former strip dancer who had just started plugging in to our home groups. She had been brought by a lesbian who one night hired her services, but then felt convicted before following through and brought her to church instead. This strip dancer had met Johnny at a fair. When the phone rang, he was afraid it was his mom and thought that if he didn't answer, she might come to his house and be the first one to find him. He took the rope off his neck and climbed down to answer the phone. The girl on the phone invited him to come to a home group that night. Since he didn't have anything else planned, he agreed to come.

Johnny was a drug dealer in our area. He was a well-known satanist with 666 tattooed on his head. That night at the home group, he experienced the Holy Spirit for the first time in his life and gave his life to the Lord. In the following weeks, he called everybody he knew and told them that he was on something that was stronger and a better high than anything he'd ever been on before—and that they needed to get filled with the Holy Spirit. He became part of our Alpha program, and soon our church was filled with his family members, friends and drug accomplices because of the transformation that had taken place in him. He was invited to speak at numerous churches in our area and became a vibrant evangelist and leader. His life was in a passionate turnaround. It was as if he were on fire, and it positively affected everyone he talked to and everything he did.

Johnny continued coming to our church for a couple of years, and then abruptly he decided to move down south. Because of his history in that area and the changes that had taken place in him, several people down there gave him a hard time. He had some enemies, and he felt harassed. A friend of his offered him a job, and it seemed like a fresh start and a good opportunity. A few months later, he was found hanging—dead.

Some mystery surrounded his death, but nothing was pursued. It could not have come as a greater shock to us all. No one in his family could believe what had happened. It was a devastating blow to all who knew and loved him. His funeral was packed with people from every walk of life, all of whom had been affected by his life and transformation.

Heartbroken, I became deeply discouraged after that. All the words of people who had questioned my decision to plant a church in this area started coming back to me: "What were you thinking?" "You really thought you could do this?" "Why would you plant in an area like East Aurora, with its history?"

I got this sinking feeling and thought, *As successful as this feels, I'm just not successful.* I remember reading about David after the attack at Ziklag. Everything had been taken, including the wives and children of David and all of his men. Yet Scripture says, "David encouraged himself in the LORD" (1 Samuel 30:6 KJV).

Feeling depleted, I asked myself, *Can I even encourage myself in the Lord?* I had to resolve that I would say, "Okay, Lord, all I have is Yours. All I am is Yours. To God be the glory." I poured out my heart. I've found that it's important when I feel that way to be honest about what I'm experiencing. I also had some pastor friends, Tom Severson and David Ruis, who really encouraged me and who were able to see and call out what God was doing even in these situations.

No Reserves, No Retreats, No Regrets

I remember reading the story of Bill Borden, heir to the fortune of Borden, Inc., the company that made millions on milk and dairy products. He spent much of his inheritance on missions, and in spite of his vast fortune and several lucrative job offers, he began preparing himself to enter the mission field. His goal was to minister to the Muslims of Northern China, but he never reached it. He saw no fruit, no converts there because he contracted spinal meningitis during his missionary preparations in Egypt and died at the young age of 25. When Borden's Bible was found, written inside it were three phrases. First he wrote "No Reserves," then later he added "No Retreats," and finally, just before he died, he added "No Regrets."

I want that to be my epitaph, "No Reserves, No Retreats, No Regrets." In the world's eyes, Borden's life might have seemed like a waste, lived in a way that was a far cry from all he could have enjoyed. But he wrote, in essence, "I gave all I had; I never backed off from the vision; I have no regrets." After he died, the Kingdom projects he had invested in completely took off. He left a huge legacy that included a million-dollar gift to China Inland Mission.

As I felt God reminding me of this story, I was encouraged to believe that no matter what, I would not live a life filled with regrets. Part of that meant determining, *I'm not going to slip. I'm going to keep my foot steady.* I walked through a dark period after Johnny's death. It was hard not to feel as though Satan had triumphed. I spoke at Johnny's funeral, and I could see so many of the people he had brought into our church, people whose lives had been impacted by his testimony. They were now walking with Jesus because of him.

It was hard to come to terms with how Johnny's life had ended, but at the end of his funeral, our police chaplain commander grabbed my hand and said, "Robby, this church is making such a difference in this city. The difference I saw in Johnny—from a Satan-worshiping punk drug dealer to who he became—he completely turned around. We have to have the Vineyard here! You can't stop!"

I was overcome with emotion when he said that. It was a huge shot in the arm for me to hear those words spoken by someone involved in so many of our city's struggles.

The Agony and the Glory

I remember being called by a single mom who was the parent of a boy in my seven-year-old son's class. She called because she knew I was a minister, and she was having trouble with her son being disobedient at school and at home. She knew that her boy saw me as someone he trusted, so I sat down with him while picking my son up from school one day. I asked him what was going on and why was he having trouble.

As any seven-year-old would do, he kept shrugging his shoulders and saying, "I dunno."

I assumed the boy's parents were either divorced, separated or had never been married, so I asked how he felt about his mom. He expressed great love and appreciation for her, so I wondered if there was trouble with an absentee dad. When I asked the boy about his father, he looked at me and said, "My father was murdered by gangs in a drive-by shooting."

I was stunned. He told me he had watched his father being gunned down right before his eyes as they played catch in the front yard of their home. The boy ran to his father's body afterward, but no life was left. Covered in his father's blood, the boy ran to a neighbor's house for help. No one would assist him because they were afraid. This seven-year-old told me, "My daddy died because I wanted him to play catch with me." I knew then that what the chief of police had said about ministering in Aurora was correct.

Many gang members have told me, "I'm only in a gang and do what I do to get respect." Many times, I've had to hold myself back from leaping across my desk at young gangbangers and shouting, "Does a seven-year-old boy have to pay the bill for you to get your respect? And what about the hours I've spent with weeping, devastated parents whose kids had been popped in the head at the price of your respect?" And yet every time a gang member raises his or her hand in my church to accept Christ, I weep tears of joy. The tension of seeing the Kingdom of God and the kingdom of darkness collide can be extremely heavy.

The Breaking In of the Kingdom

For some time, the girlfriend of a prominent gang leader in our area had been visiting our church with their son. I had prophesied to the son that if he didn't get out of the gangs, he would be dead before he could attend the next funeral. He looked at me and said, "That's just a statistic." Unfortunately, a few months later he was part of a tragic shootout that ended his life.

His mother came in to church, and I could see that she was hard. She had been through a lot. One Sunday when she attended, I preached the first sermon of my annual two-part series on sex. Every year I try to cover the biblical foundation for sex. The first week I talk about the brokenness of sex outside of marriage, and the second week I talk about the beauty of what sex is meant to be.

This woman went home after the service and told her boyfriend, "I'm not having sex with you anymore until we get married. Robby said that sex outside of marriage is sin. It breaks God's heart, and it's not the best physically and emotionally. It's better to follow God's plan."

After she blurted all this out, her boyfriend looked at her kindly and said, "You go tell that preacher that if he doesn't take it back, I'm going to go over there and pop him in the head in front of his whole church."

I know this because the woman's sister called me, crying and very upset that my life was almost over. Then the woman herself called to tell me what her boyfriend had said. She begged me,

"Please, please hide next Sunday. Robby, he's a killer. I love him and he's the father of my son, but he's crazy—he'll do this! Can't you have somebody else preach?"

I told her, "I'm not going to risk someone else's life! Don't worry about it, but don't tell anybody what he said."

I've had my life threatened multiple times. If you react, it sends a message of fear to the community and the people around you, almost empowering the threat. In this particular situation, I sensed that we needed to trust the Lord.

The next Sunday, our worship pastor came knocking on my office door. He had grown up on the streets and knew how to read situations. "Hey, Robby," he said, "I don't know if you know who he is, but there's a guy downstairs who's a pretty famous Latin King. Robby, this guy looks really jacked up. I don't know what's going on, but I could see that he's strapping. I don't know what to do." He looked at me and laughed nervously. "Please don't ask me to go disarm him!"

I told him, "No, don't worry about it, but thanks for letting me know. Just carry on as usual."

"Umm . . . okay." He flashed his easygoing grin, but I could tell he was worried. "I'm just letting you know he's here, and he's acting really strange. He's sitting on the second row."

As a fifteen-year-old, I had a gun held to the back of my head—unbeknownst to me—while sharing the Gospel. Afterward, when the man backed down and gave his life to the Lord because of my unwitting "bravery" in the face of danger, the Lord had told me, "I want you to live your whole life this way, as if you won't go one day too soon, or one day too late." Ever since then, I've tried to abide that way, trusting that all my days are in God's hands. I'm not going to live stressed or worried or fearful. To do that in our community is to fall prey to the enemy—both the physical one and the spiritual one.

I walked downstairs that Sunday and greeted people as usual. I went into the sanctuary, sat down and started putting on my mic, stealing a glance toward where the boyfriend was sitting. From where I sit on the side, I kept my eye on him. He sat through everything. We did the worship set, and then I told the girl giving announcements that I would do them today instead. A little nervous, I could hear myself racing through the announcements faster than usual. The guy sat with his head kind of turned to the side and fixed his eyes on me. Absolutely motionless, he didn't show any expression; he just watched me with his eyes.

I could feel my pulse beating against my temples as I talked. I finished the second part of the sermon on sex within marriage, the wonder of sexuality and the gift God intended it to be. When I finished, I made a call for ministry, and several people came forward. As people filed out the back, this guy started slowly moving his head from side to side. He looked down, and I wondered what was going on with him. Then he got up and slowly walked out.

Months after that man's visit to our church, the police conducted a big roundup of the twenty-three top Latin Kings wanted for murder. His was the highest count, with six murder charges to his name. At first we thought it was his brother, who had just married a girl in our church. When I found out who it really was, I called his family and asked them to let him know I was coming to visit him in prison.

They told me flatly, "You can't. There's no contact."

I told them again, "Get word to him that I'm coming; I know you can."

They told me a visit was impossible, but they agreed, "Okay, we'll let him know."

I took an intercessor from our church, and we went to the prison. As a police chaplain, I could request to see the man.

The visiting room was gray cinderblock. He came in cuffed and shackled, dressed in an orange jumper, and threw himself down on the chair. I asked the guard if we could be alone. The guard agreed, but kept an eye on us from the window.

The man's eyes looked hard. I could see the muscle clenched in his lower jaw, as if he were gritting his teeth. He certainly had the appearance of a hardened, bitter man, angry at life. He glared at me through the glass. "What are you doing here?" he barked.

"I want to talk to you," I began, not knowing exactly what I would say.

"Well, I want to talk to you!" he yelled back at me. "What did you do to me that day?"

That was not what I was expecting. "What day?" I asked.

"The day I came to your church. Did you put some kind of hex on me?"

"What are you talking about?" I asked. I thought back to the day he had visited, which had been completely uneventful. I couldn't remember any interaction with him at all.

He gave me a hard stare and said, "As soon as I sat down, I couldn't move. I was frozen in my seat. My nose was itching the whole time, and I couldn't scratch it." His eyes narrowed. "I was going to *kill* you that day for what you said to my woman."

I told him slowly, "Yeah, she told me you were after me. But it sounds to me as though God was keeping you from doing something really stupid."

He shook his head angrily. "I don't know about that. I don't know why God would want to do anything for me."

"Yeah." I nodded. "Let me tell you, He was doing that because He loves you. He has a plan for your life, and He cares for you." I started telling him the most basic Gospel, focusing on the life exchange and God saying to us, "I'll give you the life you were meant for." I was telling it in basic street terms that I thought might make more sense to him. "This is the deal God has on the table for you: Jesus offers you His life that you were meant for, that you were born for, in exchange for your life, with the direction you've taken it—the hurt, the brokenness, all the things that wound you up in prison."

At this point he broke in, "They think they know what I've done. They don't even know the half of it."

"Regardless, your life has gotten you into a mess, gotten you in this place. But God has a far better life for you, a far better plan. Here's the deal that He's offering you—the life you were always meant to live. He's ready to make that exchange right now."

The man hollered, "That deal isn't for me! That deal is for people like you and Mother Teresa and Billy Graham."

I prayed, "Lord, help me know what to say." I grabbed my Bible. "Let me tell you something. I know what you're thinking," I told him. "You're thinking that because you've done these things they're charging you with—"

He interrupted me, "They don't even know the half of what I've done."

I looked at him and then over my shoulder at the guard. "You need to be careful what you say," I told him. By Illinois law and because of Chicago's strong Catholic background, what a prisoner says to a pastor is confidential. But I also knew they were desperate to get anything on this guy that they could.

He put up his hands, "The point is, I've gone too far."

I grabbed the New Testament portion of my Bible and held it up in front of him; the rest of the book hung slack toward the table. "Listen, half of this portion of the Bible—what we call the Holy Word of God—half of this was written by a murderer. He murdered God's own people—the early Christians Jesus loved. And God chose him to write this. God offered him the deal; He's still offering you the deal. The deal is still on the table."

He looked me in the eyes, and then dropped his chin down to his chest. This hardened prisoner in front of me began to cry. Through his tears, he said, "I'll take the deal."

His brother had told me that he had never seen him cry. Even as a five-year-old, when their stepdad was beating him, he had never cried.

When the guy said those words, "I'll take the deal," I could feel a rush of God's presence in the room. It was electric. I had already felt God's presence when we were talking, but this was as if an electric wave had been released in the jail in that moment. Something broke in the atmosphere, and I was getting choked up myself.

"Let me tell you how this works. We're going to pray and give your past, your present and your future to the Lord."

He followed my lead, and as we finished praying together, he lifted his head. A *huge* smile shone from his face. His eyes suddenly looked softer, and he quickly rolled back his shoulders several times.

"Man, it's as if I carried a huge rock on my shoulders. When I prayed, it snapped off. The anger, the rage, the shame, the guilt—it's not there anymore!"

"That's the freedom God gives you," I told him. "That's the reality God gives you."

The guard swung open the door. "It's time to go back!" he snapped.

The guy jumped to his feet. "Yes, sir!"

The guard stared at me in shock, like, "What did you do to him? Is this real?"

I went to visit this man several times after that. Since he couldn't read very well, I got him a children's Bible that was easy to understand. We looked at stories in it about forgiveness, stories like Joseph forgiving his brothers and letting go. We talked about how we need to be honest and truthful.

I told him, "Your lawyers will tell you things that may not be accurate. I encourage you not to listen to your lawyers if they ask you to do stuff that you know goes against God. You need to ask God to guide you and help you know what to say. I'm going to pray with you, that you'll know the voice of God and know His Spirit and follow Him."

We prayed together every time I visited. One afternoon, we talked about the justice of God. I mentioned that Paul was known for killing Christians. At the time what Paul did was legal, but it's interesting that he spent the latter part of his life in jail.

One day this guy looked at me as we were talking about God's actions toward us. He reflected, "You know, Robby, I've got to tell my story. I've got to get my story out." He was really serious, and he looked me dead in the eye. "Robby, people don't know how far Jesus will go for them. They don't know He'll go so far!"

I could feel that it was a God moment as he was talking.

"People don't know that you can be so far from God, in the deepest pit, in the deepest, darkest place. They don't know how far He'll go for them," he said again.

I started tearing up, and I told him, "Yeah, it's like David said, 'Though I make my bed in hell, you are there, though I go to the highest heavens you are there'" (see Psalm 139:8). I looked at him. "I have to tell you, I don't want you taken out because of it. I'm worried about it. If you tell your story publicly, you could get shanked by the Kings here in jail. Or it could get you the needle. I don't want that to happen; I know God has more for your life."

He looked at me and held up his children's picture Bible, feeling flushing his face, and he shouted, "You told me they all died for this! You told me they gave everything for this. You told me that if you're not willing to spend your life for the Gospel, you won't know real life! Why should I be any different than them?" He was shaking the Bible at me. "The past few months in this stinking, rotten prison have been the best of my life because of Jesus. And if I died right now, it was all worth it!"

That hit me so hard. These weren't just words for him. I told him, "You really get this, don't you? I wish the Church got it as much as you do."

Together we prayed for God's direction in his life and situation. That was the last time I saw the man. Since then, they've moved him downstate because of his connections in our area. They could tell some communication was going on, and they were trying to get him away from his family and the other Latin King gang members. I heard later that he continued in the changes that had taken place, that he was active with the chaplain there and that he was seen as a spiritual leader among the prisoners.

Despair and Triumph

In His last heaving words on the cross before He gave up His spirit, Jesus cries out, "Eloi, Eloi, lema sabachthani?" That was a direct quotation from Psalm 22:1, and it translates, "My God, my God, why have you forsaken me?" (Matthew 27:46). This is how we know He became sin for us. He had never referred to His Father as God. Here He became fully as we are. His cry of pain and suffering is also a victory cry of dominion restored. In His moment of vulnerability, Jesus referenced Psalm 22, which foretold His death a thousand years beforehand and described the scene before Him—from the moment of Gethsemane to the dividing of His clothes. Look at a couple of the echoes of Psalm 22 that occur in the gospels:

> And they crucified him and divided his garments among them, casting lots for them, to decide what each should take.
>
> Mark 15:24 ESV

> They divide my garments among them, and for my clothing they cast lots.
>
> Psalm 22:18 ESV

> Those who passed by derided him, wagging their heads and saying, "You who would destroy the temple and rebuild it in three days, save yourself! If you are the Son of God, come down from the cross."
>
> Matthew 27:39–40 ESV

> All who see me mock me; they hurl insults, shaking their heads.
>
> Psalm 22:7

Verses 1–2 of the psalm also echo Christ's agony in Gethsemane as He wrestled in prayer, asking His Father if there were any other way to accomplish His will: "Why are you so far from saving me, from the words of my groaning? O my God, I cry by day, but you do not answer, and by night, but I find no rest" (ESV). Verses 16–17 of the psalm exactly described how He was surrounded by enemies, both the religious and sinners, and what they did to Him: "For dogs encompass me; a company of evildoers encircles me; they have pierced my hands and feet—I can count all my bones" (ESV).

The question Christ asks in that moment is one of tremendous pain, but as He calls out, "Why?" He is calling out the very answer to those who have ears to hear. In fact, when the psalmist writes this next passage, he foretells God's answer in Christ to all of humanity's question, "God, why?"

> You who fear the LORD, praise him!
> All you offspring of Jacob, glorify him,
> and stand in awe of him, all you offspring of Israel!
> For he has not despised or abhorred
> the affliction of the afflicted,
> and he has not hidden his face from him,
> but has heard, when he cried to him.
>
> verses 23–24 ESV

What appears as this triumph of pain on the cross is the breaking in of the Kingdom. It's the answer to humanity's suffering, its horror of abandonment and its need for redemption. Christ is the mediator—fully human, fully God. He entered into our suffering fully a man, but undeservingly betrayed, abandoned and condemned. He cries out as a son of Adam, "Why have you abandoned me?" It's the cry from a son to a Father. Yet as God, Christ is the very answer to that question. God has not abandoned us; He has fully united Himself to us on the cross. Identifying Himself with us in His moment of greatest shame, persecution and betrayal, Christ became a living sacrifice of love: "He was pierced for our transgressions; he was crushed for our iniquities; upon him was the chastisement that brought us peace, and with his wounds we are healed" (Isaiah 53:5 ESV).

The exchange that took place on the cross is the realm of the Kingdom I have seen break in again and again. When I was nine, I watched it break in on the face of the heroin addict in my bedroom who suddenly knew God loved him. Years later, I watched it break in on the face of the gangster before me whose months in prison were the best of his life because of Jesus. There is a reality of the Kingdom that is stronger and truer than the worst this world can do.

In His moment of suffering, Christ pointed to you and me and triumphed as the answer to humanity's cry for all time. We are not abandoned—we are His "Why." You. Me. My friend Johnny. The condemned gangster/slayer raised by his father's fists. Christ suffered so that in our suffering, in our sin, in our darkness we would know that God does not hide His face from us. And as the psalmist says, we would know that,

> The afflicted shall eat and be satisfied;
>> those who seek him shall praise the LORD!
> May your hearts live forever!
> All the ends of the earth shall remember
>> and turn to the LORD,
> and all the families of the nations
>> shall worship before you.
> Psalm 22:26–27 ESV

Everything handed over to Satan in the Garden when humankind fell has been restored to and by the rightful King. Dominion has been restored for us. Now we have to do our part of walking out the Kingdom in order to see that restoration of everything that Satan stole. Long before the exchange at the cross, the writer of Psalm 22 concluded for us,

> For dominion belongs to the Lord
>> and he rules over the nations.
> All the rich of the earth will feast and worship;
>> all who go down to the dust will kneel before him—
>> those who cannot keep themselves alive.
> Posterity will serve him;
>> future generations will be told about the Lord.

> They will proclaim his righteousness,
> declaring to a people yet unborn:
> *He has done it!*
> verses 28–31 ESV, emphasis added

Christ fully and perfectly suffered the injustice of bearing the punishment for all that was wrong in the world. In a single cry, He uttered both the agony and the glory of the psalmist's last words, "He has done it," when He proclaimed, "It is finished" (John 19:30).

Because it is finished and because He has done it, we can bring the breaking in of the Kingdom as He works through us to heal the sick, route demons and change lives forever. We can go out and do what Jesus did. *Now go!*

Me—Do What Jesus Did?

What exactly is the normal Christian life? What does it mean to do what Jesus did? In some ways, normal is still having my church roof leak. Sure, my life has changed in the past few years as I've focused on doing what Jesus did. My travel and conference speaking have increased, and I've seen an increase in authority, incredible healings and God's faithful provision. I'm thrilled to see what God is pouring out through His Church, His people and even through my sons as they are growing up and doing Kingdom stuff before they can fully speak. But when I come home, I still change dirty diapers and still have dishes piled up in the sink. People in my church still get mad at me, and I still have to work on character issues.

I don't want to disappoint you, but please don't think that if you really buy in to this—pouring out your life for Jesus and seeing the sick healed and people saved—you're somehow going to skip to a new level and avoid all the "normal" ways that God works in our lives. The truth is, there's not really a divide between the "normal" and doing what Jesus did. It's all part of His Kingdom, all part of His work in our lives. Living out the risk of His Kingdom is the invisible yeast that has to work its way through the whole dough of our lives, our finances, our marriage, our kids, our communities.

Doing what Jesus did doesn't mean that every aspect of your life is perfect. Mine certainly isn't. (Sorry to disappoint you.) I love God, I love my wife, I love my kids and my friends. I enjoy what I do. But to be quite honest, you might have read this book or heard me speak and really hated it. You might think that my theology is wrong in places, that I'm really not holy enough, that you see arrogance and pride in me or that I just tell too many jokes and am too lighthearted.

If that's what you think, you're totally right. But don't let that disillusion you. Be encouraged—if God can use *me*, He can certainly use you. He loves it when we make ourselves available, when we want Him to use us and when we press in to obedience. We have treasure inside, though we're just pots made of clay. We've each been given some treasure, some gifts, and sometimes it's just about faithfulness—that stubborn determination to keep on going on. From the natural perspective, we serve a King who came riding in on a mule, after all. But from eternity's perspective, He's riding a white horse and bringing our freedom.

The thing is to press in, and to keep pressing in and pressing up. Keep seeking His presence. Seek His presence when no one's watching. Let it infect every part of who you are—in the character choices you make, what you do with your girlfriend or boyfriend, how you speak to your spouse, the way you treat the guy at the DMV. Keep on blessing people who disagree with you and attack you. Trust me, if you think those kinds of challenges will go away the more Kingdom stuff you do, you couldn't be more wrong! But it's so worth it. The joy is there—the unbelievable privilege of being friends with such a cool God and being someone He shares His secrets with. It honors Him so much when we keep pressing in to the things of God.

For years in Aurora, we've seen people get radically saved, healed and delivered—and also radically backslide. Some of the coolest testimonies came out of tough guys who got healed and saved and led many people to Christ, and then they backslid and fell back into drugs. People we'd been rescuing would steal from us. For months at a time, people would get healed of cancer every single week in our services, yet at the same time we'd barely be able to pay the church bills. Our cars would break down; our kids would be persecuted at school. Angie and I would struggle in our marriage. I laid carpet to provide for my family. People told us we should quit, but all the while I kept holding on to these massive dreams God had given me. All the way, I was *burning* to see revival come to the Church and to the nations. And everywhere I've gone, I've seen the Kingdom of God breaking in on the kingdom of darkness. God is faithful; He is good.

But if you're looking for a shortcut, if you want to skip the character development . . . getting involved in Kingdom ministry is not the way out. There is no shortcut, no way out. If God is calling you to obedience in a certain area of life that you need to give over to Him, do it! Receive it from Him the same as you would a miracle—it's all love. It's all His amazing, tremendous Papa love for us. That love calls us toward Him, the same love that calls gangsters, calls street kids, calls to the hearts of kings and sinners and businessmen and popes alike. It's His love that heals us, that sends demons screaming out the door, that sees us, knows us and calls us by name. It's the love of the King and the beauty of His Kingdom that calls us all, just as we are, and invites us to come clamoring in.

A lot of people think Christianity is boring, irrelevant and untrue. Nothing could be further from the truth. As I said at the start, I've lived stuff straight out of a superheroes movie, except this is real. And more importantly, I've seen countless people from all around the world—young people, old people, rich, poor, prostitutes, schoolteachers, doctors, gangsters, football stars, businessmen, murderers, stay-at-home moms—accept the invitation to radically follow Christ in doing the things He did. They're seeing the Kingdom of God invade the earth as blind eyes open, legs grow out, cancer is healed, people receive new hearts, families reconcile, gang violence ceases, cities unite, Mafia leaders repent and feuds are forgiven. They're seeing thousands upon thousands of people open their eyes for the first time to experience the reality of God's eternal love and purpose for them.

This is the treasure—this is really the hidden pearl of great price—that once you get a glimpse of the beauty of the Kingdom and the reality of the richness and power of God's love, they're worth any risk. The adventure of living a lifestyle of risky evangelism, watching God accomplish His purposes through you as you step out and do what Jesus did, exceeds every sacrifice. *Now go!*

Notes

Chapter 1 Gangsters in the Doorway

1. "Aurora Homicide-Free: Illinois' Second-Largest City Finishes 2012 without a Single Murder," *HuffPost Chicago*, January 2, 2013, http://www.huffingtonpost.com/2013/01/02/aurora-homicide-free-illi_n_2396554.html.

Chapter 3 Dry Bones

1. Mario Murillo, *Fresh Fire: When You Are Finally Serious about Power in the End Times* (Port Bolivar, Tex.: Anthony Douglas, 1991).

2. Jack Hayford, *The Beauty of Spiritual Language: Unveiling the Mystery of Speaking in Tongues* (Nashville: Thomas Nelson, 1996).

Chapter 4 The Upside-Down Kingdom

1. George Eldon Ladd, *Crucial Questions about the Kingdom of God* (Grand Rapids: Eerdmans, 1952), 78.

2. Dietrich Bonhoeffer, *Christ the Center* (San Francisco: HarperOne, 1978), 38.

Chapter 5 Nickels in God's Pocket

1. My friend Tri Robinson pastors Vineyard Boise Church and is the author of *Revolutionary Leadership* (Ampelon, 2005) and *Small Footprint, Big Handprint: How to Live Simply and Love Extravagantly* (Ampelon, 2008).

2. Kevin Dedmon, *The Ultimate Treasure Hunt: A Guide to Supernatural Evangelism through Supernatural Encounters* (Shippensburg, Penn.: Destiny Image, 2007).

Chapter 6 God Speaks

1. Brother Lawrence, *The Practice of the Presence of God*, quoted at http://malianta.wordpress.com/tag/brother-lawrence/.

2. See the following references regarding what Jesus said about Scripture: divine inspiration, Matthew 22:43; indestructibility, Matthew 5:17–18; infallibility, John 10:35; final authority, Matthew 4:4, 7, 10; historicity, Matthew 12:40 and 24:37; factual inerrancy, John 17:17 and Matthew 22:29; Christ-centered unity, Luke 24:27 and John 5:39; spiritual clarity, Luke 24:25; faith and life sufficiency, Luke 6:31.

3. Colin Brown, ed., *The New International Dictionary of New Testament Theology* (Grand Rapids: Zondervan, 1986), 3:1121.

4. W. E. Vine, *Expository Dictionary of New Testament Words* (Chattanooga, Tenn.: AMG Publishers, 1995), 683.

Chapter 7 Destroying Satan's Works

1. Michael Frost and Alan Hirsch, *The Faith of Leap: Embracing a Theology of Risk, Adventure & Courage* (Grand Rapids: Baker, 2011).

2. John Wimber and Kevin Springer, *Power Healing* (San Francisco: Harper & Row, 1987).

3. Chris Overstreet, *A Practical Guide to Evangelism—Supernaturally* (Shippensburg, Penn.: Destiny Image, 2011).

4. Jack Moraine, *Healing Ministry* (Choctaw, Okla.: HGM Publishing, 2010).

5. For more on this, see Eddie L. Hyatt, *2000 Years of Charismatic Christianity: A 21st Century Look at Church History from a Pentecostal/Charismatic Perspective* (Lake Mary, Fla.: Charisma, 2002).

Chapter 8 Freedom for the Captives

1. Jacques Ellul, *False Presence of the Kingdom* (New York: Seabury Press, 1972), 13.

Chapter 9 Walking in Authority

1. John Wimber's Facebook page (administrated by his son, Sean Wimber), accessed November 8, 2012, http://www.facebook.com/pages/John-Wimber/209839175122.

2. Thomas F. Torrance, *The Mediation of Christ* (Colorado Springs: Helmers & Howard, 1992), 70.

3. George E. Ladd, *Crucial Questions about the Kingdom of God* (Grand Rapids: Eerdmans, 1954), 80.

4. Thomas F. Torrance, *The Mediation of Christ* (Colorado Springs: Helmers & Howard, 1992), 70.

Chapter 13 Perseverance

1. Pastor Bob Dawkins is my father.

Robby Dawkins has been one of the Vineyard's most sought-after speakers both in the United States and internationally for the past several years. He was featured in the hit movies *Furious Love* (2010) and *Father of Lights* (2012). Robby was born to missionary parents in Japan and had an early start in ministry. "I knew from a young age that God had called me into ministry," he says. "My parents say that from the age of two, I told people that I would grow up and be a missionary." He began a children's ministry in his father's church at the age of twelve and became the youth minister at sixteen.

Robby and his wife, Angie, married in 1992 and have pastored the Vineyard Church of Aurora, Illinois, since 1996. They felt God calling them to plant in a poor urban community, and they use "power evangelism" continuously to gather people to the church. They estimate that over 50 percent of their current attendees have come to Christ at the Vineyard Aurora, and that almost three-quarters of these have been drawn through power encounters.

"In addition to starting and pastoring this church," Robby says, "God has called me to build up and equip the local church with power tools for harvesting." The four power tools Robby refers to are prophetic ministry, healing, ministering the presence of God and deliverance from demonic power. Robby has hundreds of stories to tell about his personal experiences, which include God using him and others whom he has mentored to cause God's Kingdom to break in with signs and wonders.

Robby has been in over thirty countries around the world, helping to build the Church internationally as well as locally. He has ministered in many Muslim countries (including, according to the *Voice of the Martyrs* magazine, two of the top ten most dangerous countries). This is the purpose of his ministry International Life Corps. Robby and Angie live in Aurora, Illinois, and have six sons ages two through nineteen.

If you enjoyed *Do What Jesus Did,* you may also like...

✔Chosen